The Lost Sutras of Jesus

Unlocking the Ancient Wisdom
of the Xian Monks

Edited by
RAY RIEGERT and THOMAS MOORE

Translation by
JON BABCOCK

Ulysses Press

Published by: Ulysses Press
          P.O. Box 3440
          Berkeley, CA 94703
          www.ulyssespress.com

Library of Congress Cataloging-in-Publication Data

The lost sutras of Jesus : unlocking the ancient wisdom of the Xian monks /
    edited by Ray Riegert and Thomas Moore.
       p. cm.
    Includes bibliographical references.
    ISBN 1-56975-360-1 (hardback : alk. paper)
     1. Christianity and other religions--Chinese.   2. Dunhuang manuscripts.
    I. Riegert, Ray, 1947- II. Moore, Thomas, 1940-

BR128.C4L67 2003
275.1'02--dc21

                                                        2003044770

ISBN 1-56975-522-1 (paperback)

Printed in Canada by Transcontinental Printing

10 9 8 7 6 5 4 3 2 1

Translation of Jesus Sutras by Jon Babcock; edited by Ulysses Press

Book design: Sarah Levin, Leslie Henriques
Editorial and production staff: Lily Chou, Claire Chun, Lynette Ubois
Photographs: Courtesy of The British Library; photo of Paul Pelliot
    courtesy of Musée Guimet
Maps: Pease Press

Distributed by Publishers Group West

Acknowledgments

❦

The book you are holding came about through the efforts not only of two writers but a team of editors, designers and specialists as well. Leslie Henriques deserves a heartfelt thank you for her inspiration in all aspects of the work from conception to completion. Together with Sarah Levin, she provided a beautiful design both inside and out.

Lynette Ubois, Bryce Willett and Marcy Gordon served as a sounding board for ideas and proved to be a tough group of editors as well. Lily Chou added a deft hand to the final editing and Ben Pease contributed his extensive cartographic skills.

A special acknowledgment goes to Claire Chun, who shepherded the project from fitful start to flourishing finale, and to Jon Babcock for capturing the passion and poetry of the Sutras in a brilliant translation.

Table of Contents

❧

PART III THE SOUL OF THE SCROLLS:

Editors' Foreword

❧

Reading these Sutras is like opening a message-in-a-bottle from the seventh century. They tell a tale from ancient times and present a refreshingly new set of teachings. But the real treasure in the bottle is that the message powerfully resonates even today.

In order to convey the history, teachings and meaning of these unique scrolls, we have divided the book into three parts. The first section, "Wisdom from a Cave," recounts the 1300-year journey of the lost scrolls. Part two, "The Jesus Sutras," contains selections from the scrolls, presented in a new translation and organized by theme. The final section is called "Soul of the Scrolls" and discusses how these ancient texts relate to our everyday lives.

As co-editors of this book, perhaps the best way of explaining the diverse appeal of these writings is to recount the effect they have personally had on each of us.

THOMAS MOORE   For the past thirty years I have returned repeatedly to the New Testament, Buddhist sutras and the *Tao Te Ching* for my own continuing spiritual education. I can't imagine my life without each of these influences. I have had others as well—ancient Greek religion and Zen Buddhism, for example—but my own spirituality is at base Christian. For me, nothing could be more enriching than a highly poetic, life-energizing blend of these wisdom traditions. Hence, my excitement about the Jesus Sutras.

Personally, I will continue to pursue my birthright as a Catholic while intensifying my study of other religions. What Buddhism and Taoism have done for the Gospel teachings in these Sutras, other religions can do for each other. I only hope we continue to find more lost literatures like the Jesus Sutras that combine religions in a way that brings out the best in each of them and the best in all of us.

RAY RIEGERT   As a lapsed Christian with a passion for biblical history and Eastern thought, my fascination with the Jesus Sutras lies in the unusual saga behind these fragile scrolls. The romantic in me is completely overwhelmed by the sheer improbability of the story.

I can't recall how many times friends raised their brows in disbelief when I described the book we were writing. In each recounting I wondered when they would stop me: After the 3000-mile Silk Road journey from Persia to

China by a band of seventh-century "intellectuals?" Or as I proceeded to explain how they were actually *welcomed* by a war-mongering Emperor? The credulous let me continue on to tell how scrolls that combined three different religions were hidden in a cave for 900 years and then, upon their discovery, fought over by archaeologists from all across Europe.

The last part of the story even I do not believe: That today, a century after their discovery, these beautifully written Sutras, which elegantly weave Eastern truths into Christians parables, are still largely unknown. Hopefully this book will help bring them back into the light.

—Thomas Moore and Ray Riegert

❧

PART ONE

Wisdom from a Cave

The Writing and Discovery
of the Jesus Sutras

Wise Men from the West

❧

TWO DOZEN MONKS CLAD IN WHITE ROBES AND CARRYING icons and crosses formed an odd procession as they entered through the city gate, a massive entryway rising six stories above them. They wore beards and shaved the crowns of their heads. Their leader was a bishop named Aleben. According to a stone inscription from the era, he came "from the distant land of the Qin Empire." The distant land was Persia. Aleben and his followers had journeyed across 3000 miles of mountain and desert along the Silk Road to the Chinese imperial city of Chang-an (now known as Xian, the name used hereafter). The date was 635 C.E.

The year itself left few entries in the history books of the West. The Roman Empire collapsed two centuries earlier and Europe was mired in the Dark Ages. But to the east change was arriving in shocks and waves. Muslims were seizing the Holy Land and the Sassanian Empire

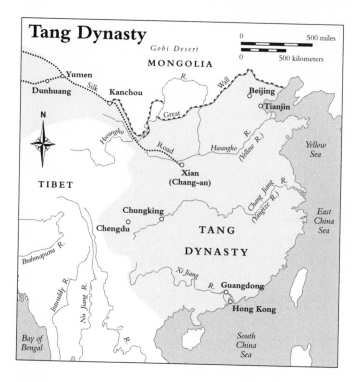

Tang Dynasty

Gobi Desert

MONGOLIA

Yumen
Dunhuang Silk Kanchou

Great Wall

Beijing
Tianjin

Hwangho Road Hwangho (Yellow R.)

Yellow
Sea

Xian
(Chang-an)

TIBET

Chungking
Chengdu

Chang Jiang (Nangtze R.)

East
China
Sea

TANG

DYNASTY

Brahmaputra R.

Xi Jiang

R. Guangdong

Irrawaddy R.

Nia Jiang R.

Hong Kong

Bay of
Bengal

R.

South
China
Sea

0 500 miles
0 500 kilometers

held a grip on the lands Aleben passed through. In China the Tang Dynasty was ushering in a golden age. Xian, located in the center of the country, was a cosmopolitan city with upwards of a million residents (the modern city of Xian actually covers only part of the ancient capital of Chang-an). Fierce warriors and a large standing army would eventually extend the empire from Manchuria to Vietnam and from the mountains of central Asia to the East China Sea. More important to Aleben and his fellow caravaners, the Chinese emperor Taizong had secured control of much of the Silk Road, making the trade corridor safe for the first time in centuries.

Today Taizong is recognized as one of China's most enlightened emperors, a warrior-statesman and to many admirers the perfect man. One of the legends surrounding him recounts how an archrival immediately surrendered after catching a glimpse of the monarch, explaining that the Emperor "has an irresistible air of being great."

Another story demonstrates how he followed the Confucian principle of "sharing the sorrows of his subjects as if they were his own." Confronted with the imminent execution of 300 men and believing people committed crimes because their rulers lacked virtue, he agreed to set the criminals free to visit their families, provided they return by their day of reckoning. His trust in the common man proved well grounded when, to the surprise of all China, every one of them came back by the fifteenth day of the eighth moon, the day of the year devoted to executions.

This enlightened despot's ascent reads less like a storybook. For almost 400 years after the decline of the Han Dynasty in 221 C.E., no emperor ruled over all China. Warlords struggling for mastery dominated the country for two centuries, and then for almost two more centuries it was divided between a northern and southern kingdom. Tribes from the steppes of Turkey and Mongolia pressed along the borders and carved out chunks of territory. In the south, dynasties rose and fell in an unsettling rhythm marked by the shock of war and rumble of short-lived truces. It was an era of petty kings and uneasy fortune; power blocs changed like the weather. The great families of China, fed by feudalism and protected by their own personal armies, filled the power vacuum as first the Han and then the Sui Dynasty rose and disintegrated.

Known originally as Li Shimin, a general in the short-lived Sui Dynasty, Taizong launched a rebellion in 616 C.E. He swept through Xian and within two years proclaimed it the capital of China, elevating his father to the throne of the newly declared Tang Dynasty. Methodically murdering several of his brothers and overthrowing his own father, he then took power into his own hands, naming himself Emperor Taizong in 626 C.E. Taizong was aided in his coup by Buddhist priests, who had been suppressed by other members of his family. As payback for their support, he reversed the anti-Buddhist and xenophobic policies of his Confucianist father and opened the door both to the West and to other faiths. Zoroastrians and Manichaeans probably arrived within a few years of his ascension; Christianity, in the form of a band of monks in white robes, came in 635 C.E.

It was not for tales of his journey that the emperor summoned the bishop Aleben to the Imperial Library. Emperor Taizong, fast forging the greatest empire in the world, was interested in a set of written teachings Aleben carried overland across Asia. The texts told of a savior who would free humankind. Taizong even provided a name for this new creed: "The Luminous Religion." Within the manuscripts themselves they are simply referred to as the "Jesus Sutras."

It's appropriate the emperor chose his library as the place to meet Aleben. Taizong's trajectory to power was fueled with blood, but he possessed a charisma and personal magnetism attractive to the finest minds of his time. The new emperor envisioned China as the civilizing center of the world. He granted foreigners the rights and privileges of Chinese citizens. Students could study philosophy, politics and the arts. Taizong took religious tolerance for granted and, "to show the world the benevolent policy of the Celestial Empire towards all barbarians," welcomed followers of alien beliefs. Monks from across Asia were soon teaching in Xian and Chinese pilgrims set out for India to collect Buddhist scriptures.

The Imperial Library, according to historian Samuel Hugh Moffett, "contained 200,000 volumes and must have been as impressive as any library in the world of that time, including the great library of Alexandria." A patron of the arts who assigned 18 scholars to create a standardized edition of the Confucian texts, the emperor immediately commanded Aleben to begin translating his scriptures. "The monks," British historian Stephen Neill recounts, "took the trouble to learn the language and to make themselves at home in the land in which they had settled." Soon they were busy rendering their sacred texts into Chinese characters.

The Silk Road and the Word

❧

THE DOCUMENTS ALEBEN BROUGHT FROM PERSIA TO imperial China (and others written by followers over the next 150 years) have never been found; only ancient scrolls containing the Chinese translations remain. Historians theorize the originals were written in Syriac, a language closely related to Jesus' native tongue. Christianity came to the region that today is Iran just a few decades after Jesus' death. One story even claims Jesus corresponded with a Persian satrap and sent a missionary to convert him. In any case, by the second century Christianity was well established in Aleben's homeland and spreading east.

The faith entered central Asia along the same track Aleben and his men followed. From Persia the route led through ancient cities like Tashkent that resonate even today with the romance and mystery of earlier times. Then the trail climbed the Pamir Mountains, the "Roof of the World," and descended into a desert wasteland many claimed was haunted. Traveled for almost 2000 years, it was not until the nineteenth century that German explorer Baron Ferdinand von Richthofen gave a name to this network of trade routes extending across Asia from the Mediterranean to China—the Silk Road.

Few journeyed the entire route. A merchant might carry goods to the border of his territory and sell to another trader who transported them along the next relay leg. Aleben and his small band of followers, carrying cargo too precious to hand off, ventured much farther than most. Their starting point in Persia was part of the Sassanian empire, a military behemoth stretching from present-day Iraq to Afghanistan and claiming Zoroastrianism as the state religion. This fire-worshiping faith, balanced between a god of good and an evil counterpart, prevailed in Gandhara and Bactria, the Eurasian-steppe areas of Afghanistan through which the pilgrims passed.

As with his original texts, no account of Aleben's trek remains. If it was summer when they crossed the desert, they would have moved by night, willing to risk encounters with the demons of the dark in order to avoid the searing wind and palpable heat of day. Like many travelers, they might have joined one of the mega-caravans, sometimes numbering as many as 1000 camels, that traveled under armed escort. Renegade warlords and bands of marauders were a menace anywhere along the trail. Sandstorms of blinding force could halt travelers in their tracks for days, remaking the entire landscape and burying them

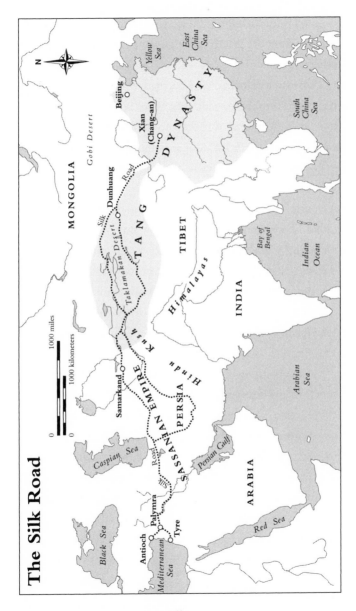

The Silk Road

in a trackless expanse. "There are no landmarks," one seventh-century wanderer explained, "so travelers pile up bones to mark the way."

Like all pilgrims, Aleben had his faith to steel his courage along the path. Persia was a Zoroastrian enclave, but Christianity tapped deep roots there. What bloomed was a different species from the religion of Rome. Christianity in the East accepted the legitimacy of other faiths and concentrated on Jesus' message rather than church doctrine. It also focused on missionary work. During the fifth and sixth centuries, numerous churches, continuously remaking Christianity into a faith fitting their own lives, spread across central Asia. By 585 C.E. the Afghan city of Herat was the seat of an archbishop. Even today ruined churches and scattered artifacts in the oasis towns of the Silk Road bear testimony to the progression of the belief eastward.

Aleben and his followers carried the word all the way to China. As Samuel Hugh Moffett cleverly remarked, "The pattern of expansion was a complete reversal of that of the missionary conquest of Europe. There the gospel moved centrifugally out from a fading Roman center to win the barbarians on the fringes of the empire. In east Asia the faith came centripetally from the barbarian outerland to reach the heart of civilization, China." No less a luminary than Marco Polo discovered traces of this very early, very Eastern brand of Christianity. Arriving in China during the thirteenth century, the Italian explorer reported finding a Christian community that claimed "the faith had already been preserved among them for 700 years."

Aleben might well have visited Herat on his way north through modern-day Uzbekistan and Kyrgyzstan. Or he could have taken the Silk Road's southern passage through Pakistan into the Himalayas. Either route led his party past terraced fields and poplar stands, high pastureland and a mountain tapestry that in their exhausted state must have appeared more an obstacle than a thing of beauty. "The roads are steep and dangerous," a seventh-century Buddhist lamented, "the cold wind is extremely biting, and frequently fierce dragons impede and molest travelers."

Eventually glaciers and talus fields gave way to the Tarim basin, a 900-mile expanse of high desert and wind-blown sand. With sand dunes rising 1000 feet in elevation, this pear-shaped wilderness was impossible to cross straight away. Caravans trekked along its northern or southern perimeter, where streams from the surrounding mountains fed a string of oasis towns. Here wild poplar and tamarisk poked out from the sand and alluvial deposits left a rich soil for agriculture.

As Persian Christians, Aleben and his band believed Mary was the mother of Jesus the man, not the god. They were captivated by the historical Jesus and treated his teachings like those of a sage. The Jesus Sutras vary even

This merchant caravan, traveling the Silk Road early in the twentieth century, shows little change from the style of desert travel of the Xian monks in 635 C.E.

more dramatically from Western Christianity. The texts that the Xian monks translated for the emperor after they arrived in China warn about the pitfalls of karma and promote nonviolence toward all life forms. To the Pope this was heresy, but even among Persian Christians the Sutras would have seemed alien.

Something happened to Aleben's party along the way, something that transformed the monks and led them to "translate" the documents they carried from Persia into a collection of "sutras" that melded the teachings of Jesus with the beliefs of Buddha and Lao Tzu. The people they met along the Silk Road and their later contact with the religions of China must have altered their world view so dramatically that when they came to render the sacred texts into Chinese, they rewrote large sections, transforming Jesus into a wise leader who saved humanity not from sin but the wheel of reincarnation.

Their first encounter with the Eastern beliefs that transfigured their writings probably began after they crossed the mountains and began tracking through the baked-mud riverbeds and crusted-over salt seas of the Tarim basin. Here in the oasis towns of the Taklamakan Desert lay a succession of petty monarchies ruled by Buddhist kings and khans. Courtiers dressed in sweeping robes fastened at the waist with belts. They sported beards, curving mustaches and cone-shaped hats fastened to the chin with silk straps. The women wore tight bodices and flared skirts embroidered along the hem. Bangles and bracelets dangled from their arms and jade hairpins adorned their heads. Cave paintings from the era portray these gaily clad inhabitants as devout followers of Buddha. Just six years before Aleben's journey the famous Buddhist monk Hsuan Tsang, passing through the region on his pilgrimage to India, was greeted by a succession of Buddhist communities anxious to share their beliefs.

These Turkic-Buddhist settlements, filled with stupas and monasteries, rested along China's western flank near the Gobi Desert. Beyond them, spaced like sentinels for over 100 miles along the Silk Road, lay the watchtowers of the Chinese empire, strategically placed to keep inhabitants in and barbarians out. Since Aleben and his men were invited guests of the emperor, they would have been greeted in this buffer zone by heavily armed border guards and guided eastward first to the Jade Gate and then across the agricultural regions of the North China Plain to the imperial capital. Here they encountered a culture steeped in the wisdom of Confucius and Lao Tzu, two other masters whose teachings reshaped the documents the monks had transported thousands of miles along "The Road of Great Events."

Like many figures in the ancient and medieval world, Aleben is more shadow than flesh, a phantom in the historical record. An eleventh-century book describes his mission: "In the twelfth year of Cheng-Kuan (638 C.E.) the Emperor Taizong had a Persian temple built for Aleben, a foreign monk." In 1623 grave diggers working 50 miles outside Xian disinterred a stele weighing two tons. Over 2000 Chinese characters were carved into the black limestone face of the slab. Dated 781 C.E., it tells of a missionary who arrived in the Chinese Empire 150 years earlier after having "read the azure clouds and divined that he should journey to the East." The stone recounts the history of the church they founded and outlines the teachings of the Jesus Sutras. It also serves as a Rosetta

Stone in corroborating historical events surrounding the Jesus Sutras and embodies similar elements of Christianity, Taoism and Buddhism.

Following the discovery, a government official sent a rubbing of the stone to Jesuits in Beijing who were soon sharing with their counterparts in Europe the story of a Christian mission to China almost a millennium earlier. Today the "Monument Sutra," measuring 12 feet in height and mounted on the back of a large carved tortoise, resides in the Forest of Stone Steles Museum in Xian. At the top of the stele two dragons bear a tablet carved with the figure of a cross rising from amid the petals of a lotus. It is an image that would have delighted Aleben: the cross of the West emanating from the flower of the East.

The Monument Sutra also mentions a monastery erected for Aleben and the other Xian monks. Like everything surrounding Aleben, this monastery and several others built for the Persians soon vanished from the Chinese landscape and memory. Even the Jesus Sutras, once heralded by Emperor Taizong as "otherworldly, profound and full of mystery," had long since disappeared. The commotion of ensuing centuries buried the last traces of Aleben and his strange texts. Like tracks in a desert storm, they might have remained concealed forever if a Taoist monk living in a town along the Silk Road in 1900 hadn't decided to clear the sand from a cave.

The Lost Scrolls

⚜

Wang Yuanlu arrived in Dunhuang about 1250 years after Aleben. Like the Persian missionary, Wang was a monk, a Taoist priest who came to the Silk Route town from his home province west of Beijing. A diminutive man with soft eyes and a wizened appearance, he was described by one observer as "a very queer person, shy and nervous." A photograph from the era captures this pixie-like figure in an oversized robe, soft-leather boots and a cap pushed back to reveal a high forehead. This air of ease and gentleness disguised a man of tenacity and vision, varied characteristics that led him first to a major discovery and then made him ready prey for European archaeologists.

Dunhuang was a vital crossroad town about 1000 miles west of Xian traversed by travelers on the Silk Road. Aleben would have passed through, stopping for provisions on his long journey to the imperial capital. Located on the border of the Taklamakan and Gobi deserts and nourished by melting snows from the Altyn Tagh mountains, this high-altitude oasis was known for its delicious fruits and vegetables and rich cotton crop. Roadside vendors stacked their stalls with pomegranates, peaches and melons; nearby stud farms bred horses for the imperial stables. In its heyday, Dunhuang was chockablock with inns, markets and caravansaries. Traders loaded their camels with fresh provisions in this "City of Sands" then followed the river with its slender strip of trees past curving dunes and angling rockfaces to the Gobi Desert or west toward "the Roof of the World."

It was not the ancient entrepôt that drew Wang Yuanlu to the region but a collection of caves a dozen miles out-

The cliffs of Dunhuang, with their multitiered cave temples, as they appeared around the time of the discovery of the Library Cave.

side Dunhuang. As early as the fourth century Buddhist monks, tunneling with crude implements, began carving chambers from the conglomerate face of a riverside cliff. Over the centuries they created a hand-hewn labyrinth with one chamber leading to the next in a series of irregular rows stacked atop each other to a height of four or five stories.

These cave temples appeared to Wang framed by a lifeless landscape of bald mountains, solitary plateaus and the spangled expanse of the Mingsha Shan, the Dunes of the Singing Sands. Like many people in China, he knew the story of the Caves of the Thousand Buddhas, how they were painted with spectacular Buddhist murals in pearl white and azure blue during the Wei dynasty and then in deep reds and blues when the Tangs came to power. Numbering over 500 chambers and stretching more than a mile, the caves are described by a present-day art historian as "among the world's most important sites of Buddhist art and afford an unparalleled overview of 1000 years of Chinese painting." Or as a fifteenth-century Persian emissary remarked, the murals are "of such character that all the painters of the world would be struck with wonder."

The Taoist monk, arriving in the 1890s, was impressed more by the sorry state of this honeycomb of masterpieces. Neglected for centuries, plaster was cracked, paint was peeling and moisture had opened fissures in the walls. Sand blown into drifts clogged many caves and soot

Wang Yuanlu, the self-appointed abbot of Dunhuang, discovered the Library Cave and devoted his life to preserving the temple complex.

from the fires of travelers had blackened paintings. The Silk Road had already been a romantic memory for several centuries and the Caves of the Thousand Buddhas were now a dilapidated stop on a deserted highway.

Here Wang Yuanlu discovered his life's work. The small monk named himself abbot and guardian of the grottoes. Nearly penniless, he plunged into the work of restoring them, traveling like an itinerant throughout the region raising funds for the project. In 1900, while overseeing workmen clearing sand from a temple cave, the priest discovered an adjoining room sealed with bricks and other materials. The hidden entranceway had been plastered over and then painted with a mural. Wang and his men burst through the plaster, tore bricks and debris from the chamber mouth and peered into the forgotten lair. As a later observer described the scene, "Heaped up in layers ... there appeared in the dim light of the priest's little lamp a solid mass of manuscript bundles rising to a height of nearly ten feet." The scrolls and other documents numbered as many as 50,000; there were silk paintings, exquisite embroideries and other priceless textiles as well as books printed 600 years before the Gutenberg Bible. Historians eventually determined that the "Library Cave" was sealed around 1005 C.E. The monk's discovery was, in the words of the J. Paul Getty Museum, "one of the most important finds in the history of archaeology."

For nine centuries this treasure trove lay untouched, protected by the arid air of the surrounding desert. Buddhist scriptures represented most of the documents, and there were ballads and poems as well. Perhaps most significant of all, the grotto contained a cache of eight scrolls that became known as the Jesus Sutras. How these unique texts ended up in a remote desert cave halfway across China from Emperor Taizong's palace is a question with no answer.

Historians do know that under the Tang emperor Christianity spread across China, borrowing beliefs and ideas from Buddhism and other Eastern religions. According to the Monument Sutra (the massive stele discovered by seventeenth-century grave diggers), after Aleben arrived in the imperial city of Xian, Emperor Taizong built a translation center, the Greater Qin Monastery, for his visitors from Persia. The first Christian church in China appeared in Xian in 638 C.E. After Taizong's death a decade later, his son Gaozong continued the work, reputedly constructing temples "in 100 cities." Soon "the Luminous Religion had spread eastward across the land."

Then the historical account etched into the Monument Sutra turns dark. It describes how "in the following years" the Luminous Religion was subjected to "rumors" and "vicious slander." Today historians agree that by 695 C.E., just 60 years after the Xian monks arrived in China, persecution of Christians had begun. With conservative Taoists and a Confucian bureaucracy in control, Buddhists also came under attack. In 845 C.E. Chinese leaders ordered thousands of Buddhist temples destroyed and directed "3000 Luminous Religion monks to return to lay life so they will not adulterate the customs of China." By the following century one observer was declaring Christianity "extinct in China." Muslims seized control of lengthy stretches of the Silk Road and in 1006 C.E. they conquered Khotan, a Buddhist city-state allied with Dunhuang. With China's borders threatened and its liberal religious tradition in shambles, historians speculate that around this time Buddhist monks (and perhaps Aleben's latter-day followers) secreted their scrolls and other sacred texts in a freshly carved chamber amid the Caves of the Thousand Buddhas.

The Archaeologists and the Monk

༄

ENTER SIR AUREL STEIN. THROUGHOUT THE NINETEENTH century Central Asia was the setting for "the Great Game," a struggle for control played out between British and Russian forces from the Siberian Plain to the mountain passes of the Himalayas. By 1900 this military maneuvering had lapsed into an intellectual contest, an international race to discover the ancient cities of the Silk Road. Archaeologists representing France, Germany, Russia and other world powers swept the region pursuing ancient artifacts and artworks to ship back to the museums of Europe. Most famous of all was a British archaeologist named Aurel Stein.

A life-long bachelor with penetrating eyes and prominent cheekbones, Stein was born in Budapest in 1862. Both parents were Hungarian Jews, but Aurel was raised as a Christian and eventually became a British citizen. He stood just over five feet tall, with a strong chin and forceful personality that belied his slight stature. Stein received his

Ph.D. by age 21, studying Sanskrit and Persian in Britain and Germany, and later joined the staff of the British Raj in India. Eventually his discoveries would lead to honorary degrees from Oxford and Cambridge and a knighthood from the British government. To the West he came to represent "the most prodigious combination of scholar, explorer, archaeologist and geographer of his generation." In China he was known as the most despicable of the "foreign devils."

China, no longer a major empire, had been carved into spheres of influence by Japan and the European powers during the late-nineteenth century. The United States declared its Open Door policy, demanding that all coun-

Sir Aurel Stein was accompanied by his terrier Dash on the 1907 expedition that led to the greatest archaeological coup of his career.

tries have an equal opportunity to exploit China's commercial potential. By 1911 revolution was sweeping the country and the next year the last emperor abdicated and the feeble nation became a faction-ridden republic.

Against this backdrop, Stein set out in 1900 and again in 1907 on expeditions to Chinese Turkestan, intent on making "a systematic exploration of the Silk Road sites." He knew treasure hunters were blindly stumbling upon priceless antiquities and believed a thorough search would net a trove of materials for the British Museum. Accompanied in his 1907 journey by his terrier Dash, the ambitious archaeologist uncovered military records in a third-century rubbish heap and proceeded to infuriate the Chinese government when he later removed the rare documents from the country. By March he was ready to descend on Dunhuang, having heard wondrous descriptions of the cave temples.

Arriving in the midst of an ice storm, a fierce desert gale known as a *buran*, Stein learned from an Urumchi trader the remarkable story of Wang's discovery of a vast hoard of ancient manuscripts. The abbot proved a difficult challenge for the British scholar. Initially refusing even to admit having found the documents, Wang next resolved not to let the Westerner see them. Chinese authorities already knew of the cache and Wang worried about spreading his secret further. Stein determined to charm the Taoist priest. He praised the reconstruction work Wang was spearheading and hinted that a donation to the project might be forthcoming. His trump card was Hsuan Tsang. The famous seventh-century Buddhist monk, whose pilgrimage to India in search of enlightenment carried him along the Silk Road, was Wang's patron saint. The moment Stein mentioned him, the abbot, "otherwise so shy and fitful ... showed a gleam of lively interest."

The Asian priest soon provided his Western guest with a grand tour of the cave temple complex. After gaining access to the Library Cave, Stein played his hand again, reminding Wang how Hsuan Tsang had taken hundreds of Chinese manuscripts from the country on his pilgrimage. Later learning that some of the Dunhuang manuscripts were translations by Hsuan Tsang himself, Stein pressed his suit, suggesting that the seventh-century monk had returned from beyond the grave to reveal the documents to Stein so he "could remove the collection to a temple of learning in Ta-Ying-kuo (England)." The Hungarian-English explorer believed he "was performing a pious act in rescuing for Western scholarship those relics of ancient Buddhist literature and art which local ignorance would allow to lie here neglected or to be lost in the end."

The monk's defenses collapsed. Succumbing to Stein's blandishments and frequent invocation of Hsuan Tsang, he decided *this* Westerner could be trusted and agreed to sell him 7000 complete manuscripts and 6000 fragments, together with ancient paintings and artifacts. Carts packed to the lip with precious documents were soon being shipped to London. The entire purchase, Stein boasted, cost the English taxpayer a grand total of $650. It was, in the words of the renowned archaeologist Sir Leonard Wooley, "the most daring and adventurous raid upon the ancient world that any archaeologist has attempted."

The next act in this European drama belongs to Paul Pelliot, a brash and brilliant French scholar who arrived like a meteor on the scene in Dunhuang in 1908. France was a late entry in the intellectual Great Game and Pelliot promised rapidly to become a major player. His entire career ran at high velocity. He was appointed a full professor of Chinese at age 22, spoke 13 languages, possessed a photographic memory, and had been awarded the vaunted Legion of Honor during the 1900 Boxer Rebellion. Earlier in the expedition, waylaid in Tashkent waiting for luggage to arrive, he filled the time by learning Uighur, the local language.

Unlike Stein, who unwittingly shipped over 1000 copies of the same Buddhist sutra to London, Pelliot knew Chinese. Ingratiating himself to Abbot Wang, now more willing to do business with Westerners, the Frenchman set to work in a space in the Library Cave left (ironically, and unbeknownst to Pelliot) when Stein removed his haul. Unrolling and examining each document, he crouched over the fragile artifacts, reading by candlelight. "I at-

Paul Pelliot, the French Sinologist, spent weeks hunkered down in the Library Cave combing through thousands of ancient scrolls.

tacked nearly a thousand scrolls a day," he recalled. For three claustrophobic weeks Pelliot worked his way through the dusty documents. Every evening he would return to his room, according to his colleagues, "his greatcoat stuffed with his most interesting finds ... radiant with joy." Pelliot's mastery of Chinese enabled him to trump Stein by selecting the rarest manuscripts. By the time the Frenchman departed for Beijing he had shipped several thousand precious documents to the Bibliothèque Nationale de France and the Musée Guimet in Paris. The cost totaled $450.

The next year the Chinese government ordered Wang's library confiscated and shipped to Beijing, but the reluctant monk hid many texts. Others mysteriously disappeared en route from Dunhuang to the capital. Adding to this strange saga, Wang sold 600 documents in 1911 to a Japanese expedition later believed to be filled with spies and dealt several hundred more to a Russian team three years later. Soon local bandits, Western adventurers and foreign traders were dealing them with abandon, sometimes delivering sacks full of rare documents to clients on other continents.

The Jesus Sutras, representing a small part of the library, became as widely dispersed as the Buddhist texts. It was not until the 1930s that they were translated into English. The scrolls themselves, recorded on parchment, were sold to Stein, Pelliot and private collectors; today a few remarkably are complete, but others are impossibly fragile, torn and, in some cases, disintegrating. After resting intact behind a decorated wall for nine centuries, they were, within a few years of Aurel Stein's expedition to Dunhuang, scattered across the world from Paris to Tokyo.

Four Scholars, an Englishman and a Pagoda

❧

ANCIENT HISTORY IS A TOTTERING EDIFICE SITTING ON A flimsy foundation. Part theory and part fact, it rests uneasily in an uncharted territory somewhere between science and speculation. The story of the Jesus Sutras starts with a band of monks whose lives are sketchily traced in a stone stele, a few imperial edicts and the sacred writings they left behind. The trail begins along the Silk Road, winds from Persia to China and then disappears for more than a millennium. Even when the track resurfaces with the discovery of a secret cave in 1900, it is soon swept into obscurity once more.

The next piece of evidence to emerge did not surface until 1933, when four Chinese scholars went searching for a monastery built by Emperor Taizong for the Xian monks. Combing the countryside south of Xian, they found a white tower and reported, "There remained by this tower a monastery in ruin and to our satisfaction we were told that this ruin was the remnant of the monastery. It was a lucky hit we made!"

Like the ancient scrolls themselves, the ruins were quickly forgotten as China was ravaged first by World War II and then the Communist takeover. It would not be until 1998, almost a century after Abbott Wang cleared sand from a cave, that the "white tower" would emerge again.

The Englishman who rediscovered this last clue in Aleben's saga first came to China in 1972. "I was 18 years old," he recalls, "and my parents and I had agreed that for a year about 8000 miles between us would be a good thing."* For Martin Palmer it was the beginning of "a lifelong love affair with China." Dabbling in his own Christian religion as well as the beliefs of the East, he soon learned about the Monument Sutra and "became obsessed with obtaining a copy of the text." Next he went in search of the Jesus Sutras, thinking they might be "a kind of Taoist-Christian Rosetta Stone of the spiritual imagination."

During his first year at Cambridge, Palmer's parents adopted a Chinese girl, binding him even closer to Asia. By 1993 he was doing environmental work with Taoist monks in China to save the Sacred Mountains, a group of holy places threatened by pollution and development. Five years later in a pilgrimage to Xian, he finally saw the Monument Sutra. Standing in "its strange protective hall, a noisy place of tourists and locals ... with the dusty light filtering in through grimy windows," Palmer gazed at the delicately carved cross that rises from a lotus flower near the top of the stele and "felt once again the astonishing power of the spirit and the pull of a long-ago time and people."

Palmer had focused on theology and Chinese studies at Cambridge and become a leading translator of ancient Chinese texts as well as a broadcaster for BBC radio and television. Both pursuits served him well during the 1990s when he made eight journeys through China to further uncover the story of the Jesus Sutras. On one of these expeditions from Xian in the summer of 1998, he headed out with a team of explorers along the rural roads of central China. According to the Monument Sutra and the imperial edict of 638 C.E., Emperor Taizong had built monasteries for Aleben to translate the Jesus Sutras. Palmer and his party—an eclectic group that included a classical Chinese scholar, a Dutch anthropologist and a feng shui specialist—set out to find one of them.

En route they passed horse-drawn carts and workers clearing boulders washed downriver during winter torrents. The track was hot and dusty as it wound to the foot of the Qingling Mountains, a towering rock wall that seemed to the BBC correspondent "like some vast curtain sealing us from the rest of the world." Here was the fabled Pass to the West, which centuries before had been the way out of imperial China. To his companions, Palmer's efforts seemed like a quixotic search for a 1300-year-old monastery that would have had to survive the wars, earthquakes and dynastic upheavals that have rocked China for centuries, not to mention the 1960s-era Cultural Revolution when most of the country's religious sites were sacked. Even more problematic, he was basing his treasure hunt on a book written in 1937 by a Japanese professor named P.Y. Saeki that described the Chinese scholars' reported discovery of the monastery. The text included an ambiguous map, possibly drawn by Japanese spies, that claimed to mark its location.

Palmer found Saeki's written directions quite confusing. In fact, the Japanese author never actually visited the site and was reporting from hearsay the accounts of the Chinese scholars. The hand-drawn map itself was maddeningly obscure: It failed to position the monastery in relation to any towns and was difficult to read. But shortly before the expedition, Palmer reports that "I got out a huge magnifying glass, put the map under a strong light," and puzzled once more over the Chinese characters that designated other temples near the monastery. This time the name Lou Guan Tai, he remembers, "leapt out at me."

In the seventh century when Aleben arrived in China, Lou Guan Tai represented the most important Taoist center in China. It was here that Lao Tzu reputedly wrote one of the masterpieces of religious literature. As the legend tells it, this revered sage, sickened by the corruption of the imperial court, was stopped at the Pass to the West as he attempted to leave China. A border guard, warned by the gods to watch out for the wise man, agreed to let him escape if he first recorded his philosophy. Lao Tzu quickly penned the entire *Tao Te Ching* and departed the next morning. He was never seen again. According to the Japanese professor's crude map, the lost monastery was not far from this sacred spot.

Palmer's quest began to assume even more of a story-book aura as he led his party over bumpy mountain roads to Lao Tzu's site. At the Taoist center there he encountered a very old woman selling cheap amulets, who told him that a nearby pagoda, Buddhist for centuries, had actually been built by "monks who came from the West and believed in one god." The pagoda (which in the translation of the Chinese scholars' account became a "white tower") rose seven stories to a height of 80 feet and leaned like Pisa's proverbial tower.

Still doubtful that this could be the ancient Christian center, Palmer climbed a hill above the precarious structure and peered through the rain at the surrounding countryside. He saw haystacks and outhouses, gardens rimmed with stone walls, smoke lazily issuing from a peasant's house. It was a classic Chinese tableau—except for one thing. Chinese custom, indeed the most elementary principle of feng shui, dictates that temples run north to south. But the ruins surrounding the pagoda below, foundations from a cluster of ancient buildings, were positioned from east to west, just like every medieval Christian church from England to Jordan.

Palmer bounded down the slope, announcing his finding with a cry. His ecstacy quickly turned to embarrassment when he was met at the bottom by a wrinkled Buddhist nun, even older than the woman he encountered earlier, who informed the excited Englishman that of course it was once a Christian monastery. In fact, she patiently explained, at the time of the Tang emperors it was the most famous Christian center in all China. Martin Palmer's discovery, which closed the circle of mystery surrounding the Jesus Sutras, had been known to the local Chinese for centuries.

This long-forgotten monastery was located 50 miles southwest of Xian, where Aleben was first received by the patron emperor. Saeki suggests the emperor chose this site not only for the Lao Tzu connection, but also because it was Taizong's "Rubicon," the place where he massed his army before seizing control of China. The Chinese government soon confirmed Palmer's findings and launched a restoration project to protect the ancient ruins. When Palmer returned the next year he found the pagoda embraced by scaffolding, with new roads etched into the landscape and frenzied work crews buzzing about the site. He also discovered that the Buddhist nun who greeted him that rainy day had died the previous month. She was 116 years old.

★ *The remaining quotes in this chapter are from* The Jesus Sutras *by Martin Palmer (New York: Ballantine Wellspring, 2001).*

Epilogue

❧

Paul Pelliot returned to France in 1909, welcomed like a hero. An entire room of the Louvre was renamed Salle Pelliot and devoted to displaying the treasures—including paintings, sculptures and rare textiles—he brought back from Dunhuang. This hero also had enemies. Soon after his homecoming, Pelliot encountered a "malevolent campaign" launched by fellow scholars trying to discredit his work.

Young, arrogant and now fabulously successful, the scholar was attacked for the haste with which he had sped through the scrolls in the dark Library Cave (feeding the fire of their assault, he had earlier likened his technique to reading at the speed of a race car). His peers were especially infuriated when Pelliot locked the manuscripts in a chamber of the Bibliothèque Nationale and kept the only key. Until Stein published his account of the Dunhuang discoveries in 1912, praising Pelliot, the Frenchman's critics claimed his vaunted manuscripts were forgeries.

Despite his petty pursuers, Pelliot went on to a brilliant career as France's leading Chinese scholar. According to historian Peter Hopkirk, he returned to Beijing during World War I as a French military attaché and told a fellow archaeologist he had "several new sites up his sleeve" but lacked funding. By the end of the war, when money was finally available, the Chinese government, stung in part by the documents lost in Dunhuang, had slammed the door on Western explorers. Paul Pelliot never worked in central Asia again. In 1945 he died of cancer, eulogized by a colleague who wrote, "Without him, Sinology is left like an orphan."

Aurel Stein continued on from Dunhuang, excavating a temple complex and boldly crossing the Taklamakan Desert. Always pressing himself farther, he later set out to chart a glacier in the lofty Kun Lun mountains near Tibet in sub-zero weather and developed frostbite. Uncertain whether he would survive, Stein traveled by yak and camel and eventually on a stretcher lashed between two horses until reaching an outpost where a missionary doctor amputated the toes of his right foot.

Far from impeding the indomitable Englishman, the incident enhanced the aura surrounding him when he returned to London. Awarded a prestigious Gold Medal by the Royal Geographical Society and receiving honorary degrees from Oxford and Cambridge, the Hungarian-born adventurer was eventually knighted. Sir Aurel Stein went on to write several books on his forays into central Asia.

A few of the 7000 manuscripts Sir Aurel Stein purchased in Dunhuang and shipped back to the British Museum in London.

He died in Afghanistan in 1943 and was buried in a mud-walled cemetery in Kabul. It would take 50 years before all the manuscripts he brought back from Dunhuang were cataloged.

Wang Yuanlu stayed on in Dunhuang, continuing to sell ancient manuscripts and other artifacts from his seemingly inexhaustible store to American, Russian and Japanese expeditions. His last years were bitter ones. Following the Russian Revolution about 400 White Russian soldiers were interned in the caves. Their fires blackened the walls and the prisoners destroyed statuary and left graffiti on ancient murals. As one observer described the scene, "Across some of these lovely faces are scribbled the numbers of a Russian regiment, and from the mouth of a Buddha ... flows some Slav obscenity." The money the Chinese government paid Wang for his remaining manuscripts disappeared en route from Beijing, leaving him ultimately with no funds to continue his restoration work. The abbot died in 1931 and was buried near the caves to which he devoted his life.

During the ensuing years the Chinese government took over restoration of the Dunhuang caves, shoring up collapsing cliffs, repairing murals and carefully preserving the complex. In 1961 they were declared a National Monument. Today the caves are a major tourist site, housing the world's most important collection of Buddhist art. Glass screens protect the paintings and visitors are led from an exhibition hall in small groups into the grottoes, which are illuminated only by flashlight. There are Dunhuang research groups at most of China's major universities. The Dunhuang Academy, established in 1944, and the U.S.-based Getty Conservation Institute coordinate much of the historical research and conservation work. The International Dunhuang Project was founded in 1994 at the British Library in London to gather all the manuscripts together again in digital form.

The Jesus Sutras, like many of Dunhuang's precious scrolls, are held today in museum collections in England and France and by private collectors. They remain largely inaccessible to the public. Since the rediscovery of the

Xian monks' monastery, the Chinese government and several international organizations have launched plans to excavate the site and build a museum beside the ruins. According to a recent report, which would have brought a smile to the lips of Abbot Wang, archaeologists have discovered a series of sealed rooms buried underground beneath the pagoda.

PART TWO

The Jesus Sutras:

Selections from the Lost Scrolls

❦

*Among the thousands of scrolls discovered in Dunhuang,
the vast majority were Buddhist scriptures. Only eight
of these precious documents were the Christian texts
that have become known as the Jesus Sutras. Poetically
written and startlingly original, they blend Christianity
with Buddhism and Taoism.*

*The following passages are selections from these
Christian sutras. They are organized thematically with
a short introduction to each section and presented here
in a new translation.*

The Ten Methods for Meditating on the World

❧

We might be tempted to read these ten laws as moralists: those people who go after money and sex don't know the truth and waste their lives. But if the Jesus Sutras are yet another example of religion urging people to flee the human condition, why bother with them? We have heard all the hell and brimstone sermons we need.

It might be better to ponder the situation these laws describe. We all like money. We all try to have a satisfying sex life. We all fail to some extent to share the knowledge we have gained. Is there some way to do it perfectly? Is the ideal life and the spotless devotee the goal of these Sutras?

It is certainly tempting to make sex or money your ultimate concern. People do it all the time. But maybe in their way they are seekers, too. Sometimes it isn't easy to distinguish an obvious reward like money from less tangible reasons for working hard and becoming educated.

If we take the Sutras as a whole, we don't find a lot of moralism. Again and again we read that the One Spirit is to be found in ourselves and our world. The Sutras don't recommend escaping this life for a more perfect and ethereal one. So maybe we should learn from the ten laws simply to be watchful when we find ourselves doing any of the things mentioned. These ten lessons make us aware of attitudes that don't take us far enough into life.

For those who think life is a game (modern people don't take life as seriously as they might), the Sutras present a law that says your spirit can be depleted through such an attitude. For those preoccupied with bank accounts, they remind us that we can't take it with us. To those of us bouncing around looking for enlightenment, the laws suggest we reflect on our hunt and how hollow the "truths" we are finding might be.

These laws are like an examination of conscience. They describe the human condition, situations we all get into, and then they spur us on to go deeper and live a more substantive life.

SUTRA PASSAGES

～

There are Ten Methods for meditating on the world that can lead us to happiness and fulfillment.

～

The first method is to realize that as soon as people are born they begin to grow old and that eventually they die. The world is like an inn where you stay temporarily. None of the beds or furniture are really yours. We will all be gone soon, for no one can stay long in an inn.

～

The second is to observe how our friends and loved ones are taken from us just as the leaves fall from a tree. Wind and winter arrive and the leaves are gone.

～

The third method is to recognize that the world is a place where the success of the mighty and the prosperity of the wealthy never last. They are like the moon at night. The full moon shines on everything until clouds appear. Or the full moon changes into the new moon and its light is gone.

∾

To follow the fourth method, consider the world as a place where people steal things from others that they believe are valuable but which eventually harm them instead. They are like moths attracted to a light who dive into the flame.

∾

The fifth method is to contemplate the world as a place where the wealthy exhaust both their body and spirit accumulating treasure that cannot help them in the end. They are like small jars that cannot hold the rivers, lakes and seas they covet.

∾

The sixth method asks you to look at the world as a place where people dally in sexual activities that bring them unhappiness instead of fulfillment. They are like a tree infected with insects that sap

its strength and eat away its core until it dries up
and breaks.

The seventh method is to think of the world as a
place where people indulge in alcohol until they are
so drunk and confused they don't know good from
bad. They are like a clear spring pool whose mirror-like
surface perfectly reflects everything. But it becomes
muddy and the images vanish, leaving filthy water in
which nothing can be seen.

The eighth method calls for thinking of the world
as a place where people act as if life were a game.
They sit around wasting the hours of the day and
wearing out their vital spirit. They are like a madman
who imagines he has seen flowers and walks around
all night trying to find them again. In the end he is
exhausted and has seen nothing.

The ninth method is to think of the world as
a place where people go from religion to religion

looking for truth but finding only confusion. They are like a skilled craftsman who carves an ox and paints it until the statue resembles the real thing. But when he tries to use it to plow his field, the ox is good for nothing.

~

The tenth method is to contemplate the world as a place where people seem to be following these principles, but are actually deceiving themselves and helping no one. They are like an oyster that holds a bright pearl. A fisherman breaks the oyster to extract the pearl and the oyster dies. The pearl looks beautiful but the oyster is dead.

The Nature of the One Spirit

❧

It is impossible to see God, the great holy intelligence, a kind of void at the heart of things, but it is possible to know God through the intelligence of things. You know the arrow has been shot when you see it flying by. You know that something sustains life because life continues to be sustained.

These are not proofs of religion or the existence of God but a way of being attentive to the source of life and meaning. The Sutras ask that we look at the nature of life and understand immediately that there is an invisible source that requires our attention. It isn't enough to become preoccupied with things. This world has, beyond its body, a spirit and soul as well. The one spirit that continues to sustain the world, sustains you. The process of enlivening is wu wei, an action that is not an action.

The Sutras ask us to be focused on life and outside life at the same time, attentive to our physical concerns and looking deeply within them for signs of a spiritual activity. The beauty of these teachings is that they come in a language that is not divisive. It doesn't lead us away from ourselves and our world, but puts us more deeply in touch with it, finding there, not elsewhere, the spirituality that provides meaning and peace.

You are not asked to subscribe to a series of truths, but to look differently, to glimpse the spirit in the ordinary life you know so well. The Jesus Sutras ask us to live in direct relation to the invisible action implied in the acts of ordinary existence. We are invited to feel the holy wind in our own thoughts, emotions and actions, and to sense it in the world outside. This creative spirit is both immanent and transcendent, both deep within life and beyond it.

A spiritual life should intensify your worldly experience, not diminish it. It should make you secular in a deep and effective way. Religion and ordinary life support each other. The more you give to one, the more you will get from the other. The more sensuous your participation in life, the more spiritual you will be. The more spiritual you are, the more intense will be your life in your body and in the world.

Heaven stands without supporting beams or posts. But heaven does not stand on its own. It does so through the power of the One Spirit, without supporting beams or posts and free of walls and fences. It is like when an archer shoots an arrow. We see only the arrow, not the archer. We see no archer, but the arrow could not have appeared on its own.

There must be an archer. This is how we can understand that heaven and earth, with the sustaining power of the One Spirit, neither crumble nor collapse, but endure because of the power of the One. We do not see this force, but we know it sustains heaven and earth. Once the arrow's force is spent it falls to earth. Similarly, if heaven and earth were not sustained by the One Spirit, they would crumble. Because of the power of the One, heaven and earth do not collapse. So the existence of heaven and earth affirm the power of the One Spirit.

Since heaven does not collapse, we know this supernatural power is something we cannot fathom. For it appears that the One Spirit created itself. Pondering this we realize there is no left and no right, no before or after, no above or below. It is a single thing, the sustaining power of the One. There is no second or third, and it cannot be made. We see the One Spirit dwelling in heaven and earth without teacher or maker. We see this force as One who invisibly sustains heaven and earth and nourishes all living things.

~

The One Spirit cannot be seen in heaven and earth just as the human soul cannot be seen in the body. The One Spirit alone resides everywhere just as the soul permeates every place in our body.

~

There is the One Spirit under heaven who lives in the divine palace of the intangible realm. This Spirit is never in just one place and is not attached to any one place. In fact, in the intangible realm one place is actually two places, and the first is the second in time. Time in the intangible realm is always seen as present, like the Holy Lord's transforming influence. It follows from this that the intangible realm has not been produced nor made. Words such as first and second do not apply. The One Spirit, therefore, is intangible, not created and not made.

∾

Do not ask whether everything that exists under heaven also resides in the intangible realm; or how it is that what we see is not created, not located anywhere and without time. Not by questions will you understand where the One Spirit is, or that the One, located in the intangible realm, has been neither produced nor made. Do not ask when the One Spirit was made or produced. This also will not be understood through questions. Not by questions will you understand.

∾

Permanent, inexhaustible; exhaustible, impermanent. The One Spirit resides within all the myriad things. The One has been neither produced

nor made, and permanently resides without end.
Among the things existing under heaven, there are
those that can be seen and those that cannot be
seen. For example, the soul cannot be seen by human
beings. Our desire to see the soul indicates a spiritual
consciousness in human beings.

~

Just as two kinds of sprouts can share one root,
human sight is of two kinds and both share one root.
We have both a soul and a spiritual consciousness.
Just as a person without a body is not complete
and a person without a soul is not complete, so is
someone without a spiritual consciousness also
incomplete. Anything seen under heaven is not
complete on its own. If it exists under heaven, it
is of two kinds, from one root.

~

If someone asks in what way the myriad things are
made by the One Spirit, or if they ask where unseen
things reside, you should answer in this way: They
reside under heaven and are what the One Spirit
sent. If someone asks how many things there are

or how many people have been made, say to them:
The myriad things under heaven all consist of the
four elements.

The Story of the Jesus Sutras

❧

The story of the arrival of the Luminous Religion in the Chinese Empire of the seventh century reads like many of the ancient texts that recount a sacred history. It is a tale full of fact and sacred myth that speaks to both earthly concerns and matters of spirit. Like many sacred stories, it shouldn't be dismissed as pure fantasy nor taken as simple fact.

As often happens in sacred history, a life-giving message arrives from a distant and alien land, a land of perfection. In this instance, the man who brought the teachings came after divining his destiny from an azure cloud, a detail that removes the teaching from the world of practical wisdom and places it in the realm of sacred space. It speaks to the soul about matters of eternal validity.

The life these teachings create sounds utopian, but again you could take this land of perfection as, poetically speaking, your ideal. Its truth, if this way of life were lived out radically as it is in the monasteries, could transform the way the world works. A life based on the deepest com- passion, not just a feeling but a posture in relation to the world, would transform our society. You could envision violence diminishing and virtue expanding.

Emperor Taizong recognized that these teachings "will save all creatures and benefit mankind." Today's "emperors" and their subjects could also find them "lucid and direct," worthy of our deepest attention, the answer to our problems. This is a gospel of radical compassion and healing. It could and should be practiced throughout the land.

The way taught and exemplified by Jesus is not one of many ways, nor is it the only way. It represents the Great Way. The *Tao Te Ching* says, "The way that can be named is not the Eternal Way." This is the deep path.

The following passage, taken from the Monument Sutra, conveys the very heart of the teaching, that the Tao of Jesus has the power to deal with the darkness of ignorance and evil; it represents the Luminous Religion. In religious circles, the image of light sometimes has a yellowish glow of sentimentality. Here light is not sentimental at all, but appears as the culmination of the teaching.

Sutra Passages

The Emperor Taizong was a champion of culture. He created prosperity and encouraged illustrious sages to bestow their wisdom on the people. There was a saint of great virtue named Aleben, who came from the Qin Empire carrying the true scriptures. He had read the azure clouds and divined that he should journey to the East. Along the way, Aleben avoided danger and calamity by observing the rhythm of the wind.

In the ninth year of the Zhenguan reign (635 C.E.), Aleben reached Chang-an (Xian). The Emperor sent his Minister, Duke Xuanling, together with a contingent of the palace guard, to the western outskirts to accompany Aleben to the palace.

The translation work on his scriptures took place in the Imperial Library and the Emperor studied them in his Private Chambers. After the Emperor became familiar with the True Teachings, he issued a decree and ordered that it be propagated:

In the Autumn of the twelfth year of the Zhenguan reign (638 C.E.), during the seventh lunar month, the Emperor issued a proclamation saying:

"There is no single name for the Way.

Sages do not come in a single form.

These Teachings embrace everyone and can be adopted in any land.

A Sage of great virtue, Aleben, has brought these scriptures from the distant land of the Qin Empire and offered them to us in the Capital.

We have studied these scriptures and found them otherworldly, profound and full of mystery.

We found their words lucid and direct.

We have contemplated the birth and growth of the tradition from which these teachings sprang.

These teachings will save all creatures and benefit mankind, and it is only proper that they be practiced throughout the world."

Following the Emperor's orders, the Greater Qin Monastery was built in the I-ning section of the Capital. Twenty-one ordained monks of the Luminous Religion were allowed to live there.

The Chariot of Emperor Taizong ascended in the West, the reign of the Tang Dynasty flourished, and the Luminous Religion spread eastward across the land.

Imperial officers were ordered to paint a portrait of the Emperor on the wall of the monastery. Here the divine presence, richly colored, shone brightly for the followers of the Luminous Religion. This auspicious symbol of the imperial presence added brilliance and bestowed favor upon the religion.

According to the Illustrated Record of the Western Regions and the Historical Tablets of the Han and Wei Dynasties: "The Coral Sea flows from the south of the Qin Empire; and the Mountains of Treasure lie to the north. To the West is the land of immortals and flower groves; and to the East it touches on the realm of heavy winds and dry rivers. The land produces fire-washed cloth, incense that restores the soul, full-moon pearls and jade rings that glow in the night. Here there are no thieves and everyone enjoys happiness and peace. Only the Luminous Religion is practiced and rulers who lack virtue never come to power. The land is vast, the culture rich and the people prosperous."

The Emperor Gaozong (650-683 C.E.) reverently continued the tradition of his ancestor and enhanced the Luminous Religion by building temples in every province. He bestowed honors upon Aleben, declaring him the Great Dharma Lord of the Empire. The Luminous Religion spread throughout all ten provinces, the Empire prospered and peace prevailed. Temples were built in 100 cities and countless families received the blessings of the Luminous Religion.

Creation

❧

An awareness of the invisible and the mysterious is the very core of religious vision. We can live fully in this life yet sense an inferiority when we confront the spiritual and realize it is unknowable and yet as important to human life as anything that can be measured and perceived by the senses.

The Sutras teach that both the earthly and spiritual realms are part of the created world and both stem from the work of One Spirit. The divine creator and the spiritual order of life remain invisible and mysterious, and we find that religion breaks down when we begin to describe it in human terms. Even the word "God" can become too familiar and lose its quality of awe and mystery. Our sacred vision becomes anthropomorphic, shrunken to human form.

The Wind in these texts is a frequent image for the divine, the creating and sustaining spirit. You can feel the wind but cannot see it, just as you can sense the invisible spiritual realm without perceiving it. It takes a special individual to imagine the invisible and the mysterious. Modern people always want tangible evidence before they put their belief on the line. They understand mystery as a puzzle to be solved or a problem to be fixed. Spirituality doesn't survive in this kind of environment.

The Sutras teach that the spirit behind our world animates people. It gives us a soul and a high level of vitality. If we do not address this invisible world, we are destined to inhabit a realm too small for the vastness of human experience. We easily become depressed from the sheer inadequacy of our imagination and are no longer animated by the spiritual and the invisible.

These passages on the nature of being offer a vision of reality that can sustain a vital human experience. They do not fall into the gap between spirit and body but affirm both simultaneously, providing us advice on how to be alive on this earth and hopeful about a life after it. They don't paint naive pictures of an afterlife but give good, simple reasons for living with a vast imagination in a world alive with spirit.

You ask of what a human being is made. People are made of that which can be seen and that which cannot be seen. You ask what is visible and what is invisible. That which can be seen is made by the power of God and consists of the four elements—earth, water, fire and air.

You ask how the four elements are made. The answer is that under heaven there is nothing that has not been created. Of the things created, there is nothing that has not been created by the One God. If the One God had not been in the world, there would have been no need to make the world. It is like building a house. First you seek a house builder then ask that the house be built. Likewise, when the One God undertook creation, once willed, it was done.

Out of love for all living things, He made himself seen in the world. Through his compassion for all creatures, the One God could clearly be seen.

Heaven and earth are the creation of the One God. The power and will of God pass like the wind over everything. His is not a body of flesh, but a divine consciousness, completely unseen to human eyes.

What the power of God carries out and what it calls forth can be known. This could not be done by any other thing. What could possibly resemble Him?

The myriad things of existence manifest the One God. Everything under heaven shares his power. Insects and animals do not understand language, so we say they do not have intellectual faculties. In classifying the myriad things, no two are the same.

Not everything under heaven can be seen. So it is that from the suspicious hearts of human beings the thought arises that other gods could have made the myriad things precisely in His image. But even if there were such gods, none could make the world precisely in His image. There are two kinds of things, the visible and the invisible, and it is clear the One God made them both.

~

People are of two natures. If they were of one kind, nothing more could be said. If there were not two natures, how could God make this thing called a human being? Everyone under heaven is divided in accordance with this divine truth of the two natures—body and spirit. One God makes both.

~

In finding the One God, we discover that two worlds have been made. In the world of the body we suffer demise and death, but in the world of the spirit we are permanent and secure. The spirit, the soul, is immortal. The power of God energizes both body and spirit.

Biblical Parallels

❧

One part of religion involves moral guidance. We all need simple instructions for conducting our daily lives with sensitivity toward others. We require motivation and ideas for living with a sense of justice and common need. Sometimes moral instruction is overdone. People lose the joy of life and become laden with a weight of guilt. The depth of religion is lost under a thick overlay of moralism and righteousness. What we need is an ethical compass that affirms life without banishing pleasure and innocence.

The moral guidelines found in the Sutras have this quality of lightness and moderation. They clearly echo the teachings of Jesus in the New Testament. Here they have a simplicity and quality of common sense that keeps them livable.

Morality is not so much a set of principles as a way of life that provides a level of belonging and offers security and community. The golden mean, "Act toward others as you would have them act toward you," expresses the mysterious fact that we are all profoundly dependent on one another, all mirrors of each other, and all somehow participants in the same life. This is not just moral principle; it is the secret to living with joy and pleasure.

Moral instruction often becomes wordy and complicated. But in these biblical echoes from the Jesus Sutras we discover a succession of pithy and insightful gems. To keep our morals in mind during daily activities, we need simple, short and workable ideas. Religion must be an art of memory, allowing us to live from our ideals in the most demanding and complicated situations. These sayings are the tools of that art, interior flash cards to keep us honest and open-hearted.

The Jesus of the Gospels is a master of humane moral teaching. In these Sutras, the inherent simplicity of his lessons shines brilliantly, and their fresh, sparkling language renews our moral wisdom.

SUTRA PASSAGES

When you give, do not give in front of others out of respect for the World Honored One, the Good Spiritual Friend. If you give with your left hand, do not let your right hand know it. When worshiping, do not let others hear or see or know about it. Your worship is for the One Spirit alone to see.

Forgive all others and in this way you will be forgiven for the evil deeds you have done. Also remember to forgive yourself. For just as you forgive, so does the One Spirit forgive you. By forgiving others you will be forgiven.

Do not pile up treasures on the ground where they will rot or be stolen. Treasures must be stored in Heaven where they will not decay or be lost.

In the human world there are two kinds of life:
The first is to live for the One Spirit; the other is to
pursue riches. Don't worry about acquiring wealth or
whether you will have enough to eat and drink. You
are not like a newborn babe who can be attacked by
thieves and left with nothing.

I say to all of you: Seek only one thing. Pray to the
One Spirit and you will be without blame. Whatever
clothing you need, you will receive. Do not worry
about drink, food or clothing.

The One knows your needs.

～

Look at the birds in the air. They don't plant
or harvest, they have no barns or cellars. In the
wilderness the One Spirit provided for the people
and will also provide for you. You are more important
than the birds and should not worry.

～

Do not look for bad qualities in people. Seek the
best in others and learn from them how to be good.
If you have a beam stuck in your own eye, don't turn
to someone else and say, "You have something in your

eye which I will remove." Don't be a hypocrite; first take the beam out of your own eye.

∾

Always tell the truth. Do not give pearls to swine; they will trample and destroy them. You will only be blamed by them for your actions and incur their anger. Why don't you realize this yourself?

∾

Knock on the door and it will be opened for you. Whatever you seek, you will obtain from the One Spirit. Knock on the door and it will be opened for you. If you pray and do not get what you want, it is like knocking on a door that is not opened. This means that what you requested is harmful to you. If you go to your father and ask him for bread, you will receive it. But if you ask for a rock, it will not be given for fear it will hurt you. To ask for a fish is permitted, but if you ask for a snake it will not be given to you because it could bite you.

∾

Whatever you want from other people, they will also want from you. So whatever other people do for you, you should do for them.

～

Do not take advantage of people weaker than you. If you see a poor child, do not turn her away. Give food and drink even to your enemy and by doing so rid yourself of hate. When you see a man struggling with his work, help him and provide him with something to eat. Seeing someone naked, give them clothing.

～

If a poor child asks for money, give what you have. If you have nothing, explain that you have no money to give. Do not laugh at the sick for they did not bring illness upon themselves willingly.

～

Do not ridicule a naked child or one clothed in rags. Do not cheat others out of their property or oppress them. If someone stands accused, reflect on the facts and judge them fairly. If those with no family to support them stand accused, consider the circumstances and do not treat them wrongfully.

~

Do not be arrogant or boastful. Do not make up stories or incite people to fight with one another. Those who abide by these precepts do not harm others.

~

With respect to all other living creatures, always act kindly and never think cruel thoughts. By acting this way, there is less cause for regret. May each person always do what is good for all other living creatures.

The Four Laws of the Dharma

❧

No desire, no action, no virtue, no truth: these are four laws worth pondering. We have already seen there is a kind of desire that clouds the soul and interferes with spiritual perception. This is obsessive desire, not the simple and deep desire that is often a trustworthy signal of soul. Know your deepest desires and you know what your deepest soul wants. Nothing is more precious than that.

Obsessive desire is different. The compulsive nature of this wanting makes it neurotic, desire that is repetitive, stagnant and fruitless. Desire needs deep and healthy roots that reach down to a level where it expresses a genuine need. Real desire tells you what is missing or where your life needs to go next. Superficial desire obscures those roots and can even damage them. It prevents us from dealing with our depths and making necessary changes.

Action, similarly, is either shallow or deep-seated. It can be doing for the sake of doing, busyness that gets nothing done. Today we believe more in being busy at something than in really accomplishing anything substantive. Much of our cultural activity prevents us from doing what needs to be done. Government makes all kinds of laws and spends great sums of money just being busy but rarely tackles the deep needs of the community. Business does the same without providing the things that lead to peace and creativity. We need a kind of doing that is not mere activity.

The Sutras' words on virtue make it clear that good deeds should not be for personal pride. We live in a narcissistic period, a time of insecurity, of worry about self and ego. It takes a special effort to do good in the world without trying to prop ourselves up with good deeds.

Today the notion of truth is competitive. Even in religion, one group sets itself above another with its claims of knowing the truth. One wonders if we shouldn't just abandon the word altogether, since it has caused so much trouble. It takes a strong sense of self simply to observe the world with insight and precision, without bringing the ego into the picture and claiming ownership of your ideas.

These four laws offer liberation from self-consciousness, anxiety and competition. But to put them into practice requires a level of personal emotional security and maturity that isn't easy to achieve in an age of anxiety.

SUTRA PASSAGES

~

A follower asked, "You said that no desire, no action, no virtue, no truth are the Four Laws and the Way to Peace and Joy. But I do not see how there can be joy when there is no existence."

The One Lord, the Messiah, answered, "What a wonderful question. I will tell you again. It is only nothing that can give rise to something. If it were in something, Peace and Joy would never be. And why? Take for example a mountain filled with forests. The leaves and branches of the trees spread shade everywhere. Surely this mountain forest does not seek birds and animals, but they all come here on their own to nest and gather.

"Or think of a great sea that draws all the rivers and springs and is vast without limits and deep beyond measure. Surely this ocean does not seek fish and scaly creatures. But they all dwell there on their own.

"Those of you who seek Peace and Joy are like these birds and fish. You need only pacify your minds and live quietly. Then in practicing these teachings, you will not have to seek Peace and Joy, they will simply be there like the forest and the ocean. This is how nothing gives rise to something."

~

The first law is no desire. Your heart seeks one thing after another, creating a multitude of problems. You must not allow them to flare up. Desires are like the roots of plants. Since they are buried deep below the earth you can't see them and don't know they are damaged until the buds of the plant begin to wither and die. Desire in the human heart can't be recognized from the outside either. Desire can sap wholesome energy from the four limbs and the body's openings, turning it into unwholesome activity. This cuts us off from the roots of Peace and Joy. That is why you must practice the law of no desire.

~

The second law is no action. Doing things for mundane reasons is not part of your true being. You have to cast aside vain endeavors and avoid shallow experiences. Otherwise you are deceiving yourself.

It's like being aboard a ship adrift on the ocean. The sea water rolls and swells with the wind, creating waves that force the ship this way and that way. There is no peace on board, everyone is worrying they will sink. We live our lives veering this way and that: We do things for the sake of progress and material gain, neglecting what is truly important and losing sight of the Way. That is why you must distance yourself from the material world and practice the law of no action.

∽

The third law is no virtue. Don't try to find pleasure by making a name for yourself through good deeds. Practice instead universal loving kindness that is directed toward everyone. Never seek praise for what you do. Consider the earth. It produces and nurtures a multitude of creatures, each receiving what it needs. Words cannot express the benefits the earth provides. Like the earth, you are at one with Peace and Joy when you practice the laws and save living creatures. But do it without acclaim. This is the law of no virtue.

~

The fourth law is no truth. Don't be concerned with facts, forget about right and wrong, sinking or rising, winning or losing. Be like a mirror. It reflects one and all; blue, yellow and all other colors; long, short, any size. It reflects everything as it is, without judging. Those who have awakened to the Way, who have attained the mind of Peace and Joy, who can see all karmic conditions and who share their enlightenment with others, reflect the world like a mirror, leaving no trace of themselves.

Jesus' Teachings for Those
Who Have Escaped the Realm of Desire

❧

Here we arrive at one area where the highly spiritual teaching of Buddhism and Taoism run up against the more engaged teaching of Jesus found in the Gospels. The accent on purity in this section can be taken as an example of leaning too far into the spirit and away from the soul and body. Still, there is a way to read these teachings that keeps the spirit grounded and the soul deeply connected.

In fact, the section opens with the fascinating statement that the Higher Dharma, which at the end we understand is our original nature, "lies buried and cannot be seen." It is deeper than ordinary perception, and therefore we have to look far into ourselves and our lives to find this spirituality. It is a spirituality of depth.

But our circumstances can be cloudy. We may not see the spiritual nature of our ordinary lives. Somehow we have to clear away our vision. In Greek literature, this process is called catharsis, a process of cleansing that can be accomplished through language and imagery. This is different from trying to figure it all out rationally. Such an effort of reason and ego doesn't achieve the clarity needed to glimpse the spirit in the ordinary.

Desire moves in two directions: it can be a craving, an excessive feeling of need akin to the intellectual struggle to find meaning. Or it can be a deeper, more heartfelt longing. It need not be full of ego. It is the egotistic need for knowledge and success that obstructs the path toward your original nature. This Jesus says, "When you are not moving and have no wants, you do not seek." Maybe he also teaches desire without desiring; that is, a certain kind of desiring that isn't heroic and needy.

Our struggle to know and our wish for success and happiness both need to be emptied, thinned out so they take us to the mysteries deeper than our eyes. The Law of life is not a literal set of rules and teachings, not a literal organization, not a literal style of life. This Law is your heart, your nature. Know that, and you discover the secret of spirituality.

Don't try to arrive at a mental understanding of all this. These Sutras recommend being like an animal. You are an animal not only in the usual meaning, having instincts and a body, but having the soul of an animal. You don't have to do more than be yourself. But it isn't always easy to be yourself, with all the spontaneity and immediacy of an animal. Your efforts and thoughts will get in the way. You have to realize that the teaching you seek is the truth of your very nature. When you find it, you will recognize it because it has been there all along.

SUTRA PASSAGES

⁓

All creatures seek the Higher Dharma. They long for the Way of Peace and Joy, which lies buried and cannot be seen.

⁓

The truth is like the moon reflected in water. When the water is stirred up and muddy, the image of the moon does not appear. And it is like a fire in the grass. When the grass is wet, we do not see light. So it is with the all of us when the spirit is clouded.

⁓

Everyone who wants to practice the Higher Path must first get rid of movement and desire. When you are not moving and have no wants, you do not seek and do not act. When you do not seek or act, you can be pure and still. As you become pure and still, you will gain insight, and when the insight becomes omniscient and omnipresent you will experience Peace and Joy.

~

We are always seeking and acting and because of this we create movement and desire, which cause unhappiness and make it difficult to attain Peace and Joy. Therefore, I say we should live without desire and action, apart from the evils of the world. In this way we will enter into the source of what is pure.

~

Release yourself from the bad things of the world and seek what is pure. Purity is like empty space, it produces the light of love whose brightness illuminates everything. Because it illuminates everything, it is called the Way of Peace and Joy.

~

I dwell in all the heavens and in all the earths, sometimes in the path of gods, sometimes in the human realm. I save those who are being punished for their actions. But nothing is ever heard about their salvation because it is like empty space, without attachment or any mark of merit. Why is that? Wherever there is merit, there is fame; and whenever there is fame, we consider ourselves different from others. This clouds our minds and leads to self-pride, which prevents us from attaining Peace and Joy and the state of perfect understanding.

∾

Those who have compassion for other creatures and act in this way without seeking praise are true to their own hearts. They possess spiritual and psychic powers that guide them to what is right and important. Ultimately it leads them along the Way of Peace and Joy to enlightenment.

∾

I see the Dharma, my vision is not blocked by forms. I hear the Dharma, my ears are not overwhelmed by sounds. I smell the Dharma, my nose is not filled with scents. I taste the Dharma, my tongue is not deceived by flavors. I move with the Dharma, my body is not hindered by physical forms. I know the Dharma, my mind is not cluttered with things. Once you embody these six Dharmas, you will understand the Teaching.

Truth cannot be verified. And why? If we speak of truth, then in speaking of it our minds are obstructed and we move further away from it.

Avoid self-praise. Try to disengage from words. Be compassionate toward the weak and help them eliminate their boundless desires. In this way you can help them transcend the lesser truths and attain the Highest.

If you listen to these Sutras and take pleasure in them, if you read them aloud and carry them in your mind, you will plant strong roots for many generations to come. Your father and grandfathers, your mother and grandmothers, who cherished these teachings and found joy in them before you, have created a tradition you are continuing.

The Sutras are like the spring rain that waters everything, giving life to buds and roots. Without the rain the roots would never grow. In studying them you are enjoying the fruit that earlier generations planted for you.

~

Someone who is about to enter the military needs armor to protect himself. It must be strong so he doesn't have to worry about being attacked. It is the teachings of these Sutras that protect people as armor shields a soldier.

~

Anyone who crosses the ocean must have a boat before taking on the wind and waves. But a broken boat won't reach the far shore. It is the Sutras of the Luminous Religion that enable us to cross the sea of birth and death to the other shore, a land fragrant with the treasured aroma of Peace and Joy.

~

Consider someone who discovers an epidemic that is causing the multitudes to sicken and die, and then learns of a precious incense whose fumes can recapture the soul and bring the dead back to life. So do these Sutras of the Highest Law of the Luminous Religion enable people to recapture their lives, eliminate suffering and gain true wisdom.

∼

The Sutras are like a great fire burning upon a high mountain. The light from that fire shines upon all.

A Parable

❧

Many people have a narrow reading of the Gospel, saying that Jesus is the way, the truth and the life. They take it to mean that if you're not Christian, you can't know the truth of things. But those words are open to another reading entirely. Jesus is a way toward living without the nervous, egotistic effort these Sutras consistently warn against. His teaching offers an effective way to find what you are seeking, even if you don't know what you're looking for.

The man in the parable wants what the mountain represents. But he, like all of us, is crippled. He needs help. This may sound like an obvious condition, but you have to step back sometimes and remind yourself that in spiritual matters you can't go it alone. Throughout history, people have come together to assist each other in seeking and establishing a spiritual identity.

In the parable, the Good Spiritual Friend is the ladder that allows us in our crippled state to ascend the mountain. In this context, the relative is Jesus, but he may appear in the guise of an ordinary friend or even an interior realization. It's significant that compassion and knowledge are linked in this fashion. Spiritual knowledge, as the Sutras say again and again, is awareness of the heart. When your heart is open, you know things you can't understand when your heart is closed. There is an intelligence of the heart, a knowing that comes only when you are capable of profound compassion.

Let's not overlook the detail that the compassionate one who serves as a helper is a relative. This is not some religion or teaching outside your nature and your world. It arises from deep within your context, from the life you lead and the people you know. It is a hidden mystery and the purpose of the Sutras is to unveil the secret. That is why you are instructed to read the Sutras as often as you can, so that you will keep in mind these secret ways of finding yourself.

∼

The Messiah told a story: There was a bejeweled mountain with groves of jade and pearl-like fruit that glistened and cast light in the forest. Lovely and aromatic, the fruit could satisfy any hunger or thirst and cure any illness.

A sick man heard about this mountain and began yearning day and night for its precious fruit. But the mountain was high, the road was long and he was weak and crippled. He yearned to go but could never fulfill his dream. Finally he asked a close relative, who was wise and capable, to make ladders and cut steps in the mountain. By pulling and pushing the man, the relative was able to take him to the summit where the sick man was immediately healed.

Many people who yearn to climb this peak are confused and worried. They want to enjoy the pearly fruit that grows on the Mountain of Peace and Joy, but their passion and faith are nearly exhausted. If they rely on the Good Spiritual Friend to be their relative and the teachings of the Sutras to be their ladders and steps, they will awaken to the Way and follow it to the summit.

The Five Skandhas

❦

The following passages develop the idea that human life is both physical and spiritual. Western theology might say that we are incarnated souls, having a vast spiritual identity while living a fully bodily existence. The Sutras spell out this mystery of incarnation somewhat differently. Body is to the soul as fire is to the sun. Both are essential.

We live in a culture that operates as though we were pure fire and that there was no sun, no soul. We trust science because it proves its insights through practical results. We may think about soul and spirit in church or temple one day a week and then live the rest of the time in a materialistic universe. The Sutras offer a way to get out of this splitting of sacred and secular. They insist on the necessity of both body and spirit.

They go further by saying that the soul is the sculptor of our experience. The tendency of the modern person is to explain everything on a horizontal plane. We are who we are because of our childhood, because of our common history. The world we live in is the result of natural evolution and cultural development. We believe in this dynamic horizontal movement.

But the Sutras speak for another level altogether. They affirm both body and spirit. They recognize a soul between these two, a soul that shapes our experience. Out of this vision they imagine an eternal life, something that a purely secular, materialistic philosophy cannot do.

There is no need to take this philosophy naively as though you were not a sophisticated modern adult. You don't have to entertain simplistic notions of a heaven and an afterlife. It is sufficient to have a vision of life that surpasses the materialistic notion. You can live as though you are eternal. You can tend your spirit and soul, just as you tend your body, and over time you will find a special tranquility and depth of meaning.

These particular sutras contain a phrase full of significance—"the soul wants to be clothed in a body." This is a good way to see the human body and the physical world. Deep within the most ordinary experience, the soul is at work. Nothing can be explained in purely physical terms because life is always a manifestation of the physical life of the soul. Everything we do has a karmic quality and is an expression of soul, and all our actions relate to each other. Everything we do affects who we are, and so we might be advised to take care in the way we treat ourselves, our world and our fellow human beings.

SUTRA PASSAGES

∾

The body and soul are manifest in the five skandhas [forms, feelings, perceptions, impulses, consciousness] and are linked through the skandhas. There is no eye that does not see, no hands that do not work, no feet that do not walk. So are the body and soul combined in the skandhas. It is like the interdependence of the sun with fire, two things that make one phenomenon. Fire comes from the sun but the sun does not burn; it needs fire to burn. Fire cannot burn or create light without fuel. So fire does not have its own light; it requires fuel to create light. They each depend on the other. If the sun and fire were the same thing, then the sun would burn of itself and produce light. But it cannot burn or create light without fire. We find identity in difference and difference in what is the same. All this is done by the power of the One God.

∾

The five skandhas help perfect the soul. They dwell in the world always and affect the soul of all living things. They are like the soul's clothing. They are the flavors of the soul; through them the soul recognizes the image of God. As the teaching says: When the soul is in the body it grows like a seed of grain grows when planted in the ground. When it is stored in a cellar after being harvested, the grain no longer has water or manure to sustain it, but it will still sprout upon contact with a warm breeze. So the soul within the body does not seek out food or drink or require clothing, but through the skandhas continuously renews itself.

~

When heaven and earth come to an end, the souls of the dead will come back to life through the five skandhas. But at this time the soul will be sufficient unto itself. Free of the body, it will not need clothing and food but will dwell in permanent bliss, using its psychic powers. The bliss of that world is the happiness of the soul playing in the body without the limitations of the physical world. The carefree and blissful state of the soul in that world is due to the power of the Lord of Heaven.

If the Lord of Heaven is deeply respected, all things will be clearly seen and what you need will be given to you. When the soul wants to be clothed in a body, the five skandhas will ensure that it can live permanently in the world.

A New Way of Life

ఴ

The *Tao Te Ching*, the central text of Taoism, says, "The way that can be named is not the Eternal Way." The religions of the world offer many ways to deal with desire and evil, but what is important in every case is the deep method, that which lies within all the various approaches to spirit.

The following selections from the Sutras give a sweeping and brilliant summary of the teaching of Jesus, showing that the Eternal Way can be found there. He created the world and with infinite care offers a way to be in it with virtue and benevolence. He is both the Creator and the Compassionate One.

Since this way of Jesus deals effectively with ignorance and evil, it is called the Luminous Religion. Today many spiritual people use the image of light to describe their discovery of meaning in existence. But sometimes their references to light sound sentimental. After all, life is made up of both the dark and the light. The Jesus Sutras never come across as sentimental. They make it clear that the Luminous Religion is an intelligent, complex and subtle philosophy, a blend of the challenging lessons of Jesus with the awesome, crystal-clear teachings about Buddha and the Tao.

The Tao is the law that lies deep in the nature of things, where desire and effort are stilled. There you find strength in yielding and substance in spiritual emptiness. It is a law in which contradictions are reconciled. There is no way you can live this law and at the same time participate in the egotistical struggles of success and identity that are so much a part of the superficial goals of modern culture. You can live in this world without participating in its anxious values, but to do so you have to keep in mind the primary virtue of compassion.

The Sutras speak of the Way as a raft of salvation and compassion. The image echoes an ancient idea that Buddhism is a raft, either great (Mahayana) or small (Hinayana), ferrying you across the choppy waves of human existence. This new raft is the Way offered by Jesus, an effective means of deliverance from ignorance and anxiety. Concern about status and desire for personal success get in the way of compassion, so you need a point of view that is not rooted in anxiety.

Following Jesus explicitly, that is, externally and in name alone, doesn't offer the deliverance promised. You have to find the Eternal Way, the Luminous Religion that lies deep within spiritual practice and teaching. The Sutras make it clear that only this eternal, archetypal way is effective.

❧

Who has seen God? No one can see God.
The face of God is like the wind. Who is able to
see the wind? Always present, God never stops
circulating throughout the world.

❧

People can live only by dwelling in the living breath
of God. Only in this way can they be at peace and
realize their aspirations. From sunrise to sunset, they
dwell in the living breath of God; every sight and
thought is part of that breath. God provides a place
for them filled with clarity and bliss and stillness. All
the Buddhas are moved by this wind, which blows
everywhere in the world. God resides permanently in
this still, blissful place; no karma is done without God.

❧

No one really knows how the wind moves. They
hear its sound but cannot see its form. No one sees it
as straight or upright; it is not yellow, white or blue.
No one knows where it comes from.

Many people believe their gods are like the Lord of Heaven. They claim their writings are holy and joyous. They say they have a different Lord of Heaven. Many of these beliefs are very old and each faith has its followers.

The Lord bestows great wisdom upon people. To repay the loving kindness, we must take stock of our karmic debt, think it over carefully, and realize that we will attain heaven only by avoiding what is bad and unwholesome. May all people do what is good and ponder what they have done.

Whoever is born will die. All living creatures are destined in this way. Our lives are created by the wind. As the life-force diminishes and death draws near, the wind leaves our bodies. Our hearts and minds are not really ours but live because of the wind. When the wind leaves someone, their life comes to an end. No one can see when the wind will depart. No one can know the face of the wind or whether it is red or green or some other color. Because we cannot see the wind we ask, "Where is the Lord of Heaven." And we question why we can't see him. But how can someone living on earth be able to see the Lord of Heaven? The Lord is not the same as a person, so how could someone see him? There is no one who can fully know the Lord of Heaven.

People must first ponder their own karma. Only after the Lord of Heaven suffered horribly was he able to help save others from karma. Living creatures are similar to Buddha and can work toward their own salvation.

Whoever receives God but continues to do what is unwholesome or incites others to act in this fashion has not received the teachings of the Lord of Heaven. Such a person will abruptly plunge into the path of rebirth and be consigned to Yama, King of the Hells.

~

God's knowledge is true knowledge, it is different from what is known in the world. It preceded the knowledge of the world and will endure eternally.

~

Do what you have to do here on earth and your actions will determine your place in the next world. We are not born to live forever in the world, but are here to plant wholesome seeds that will produce good fruit in the world beyond this one. Everyone who seeks the other world will attain it if they plant good seeds before departing.

~

There is a teaching that says, "Do what is good." In addition to being true to the Lord of Heaven, we must always do what is good. When we lack mindfulness, we are like someone who builds a house out of ignorance, neglecting to set the foundation firmly in the ground. The wind comes and blows it away.

Prayers

❧

The beautiful and poignant blend of Eastern and Christian images that is the heart of these Sutras gives a degree of personality and relatedness to otherwise abstract ideas. It is one thing to speak of the Way and the nature of things but another to have the personal figure of Jesus embodying this wisdom. Here you can pray to the teacher of wisdom and praise his way of life as it models ancient teachings.

The Sutras include prayers of praise, petition, wonder and awareness. They let us shift from spiritual study and reflection to ritual. Many teach the mysteries of a life dedicated to profound, selfless engagement. With these prayers we bring our emotions forward and enter directly into that life with petitions and praises.

Prayer is an important form of expression and articulation that may seem out of place to many in a modern setting. Today people ask, how does prayer work? Is it worth praying in a time when many pious religious practices are dismissed as superstition and outmoded magic? The Sutras convey extremely subtle insights into the nature of human experience. Their intelligence is palpable on every page. Perhaps these few prayers will come across with equal intelligence. Yes, you can pray today, and yes, your prayer will be effective.

Prayer shifts reflection from one-sided contemplation to two-sided dialogue. You don't have to know how this special dialogue works. To address the mystery of existence as a person is to enter life with your whole being, without being protected and defended by distance. Now you can address the core of existence through the personality of Jesus, without any surrender of your sophistication. In fact, in a so-called post-modern world, it makes more sense than ever to speak in dialogue with the mysterious foundation of existence. You don't have to know the mechanics of what you are doing, you only have to surrender your skepticism and enter the dialogue with intelligence and an open heart.

～

The highest heavens revere You.

The great earth remembers the peace You have bestowed.

Man's original true being looks to You as its ultimate refuge.

You, Loving Father of the Three—heaven, earth, mankind—Aloha.

～

All good creatures worship You sincerely.

All intelligent beings praise You in song.

All who hold what is real take final refuge in You.

Your holy light of love protects us from the demons.

Impossible to know or attain are Your Rightness, Reality and Permanence.

～

O Loving Father, Enlightened Son, Holy Spirit King,

You are the Monarch of monarchs.

You are the Dharma Sovereign among all the World Honored Ones.

But not through our eyes can we see Your visage.

You alone bind together all that is good, You of absolute purity.

You alone are the spiritual power, You of unsurpassed strength.

You alone do not revolve on the wheel of birth and death, You of the eternal spirit.

You are the root of all that is good; this can never be changed.

Everything good flows from your compassion.

We marvel at the sublime joy You radiate in our kingdoms.

O Messiah, Universally Honored Son of the Great Sage,

May You take humankind from the world of suffering and save us all.

King of Eternal Life, Lamb of Love and Bliss,

Who never shirks the toil of saving the suffering,

We pray You undo the bad karma of all who are born.

Allow us to discover our true nature in goodness and free us from our troubles.

Holy Son, who sits to the right of His father's throne,

A throne that exceeds all others, unequaled in its awesome height,

Master, we pray that You hear the poor, answer their multitude of requests,

And lower rafts for them so they can float beyond the burning stream.

O Teacher, You are our Loving Father.

O Teacher, You are our Holy Master.

O Teacher, You are our Dharma King.

O Teacher, Your strength can save us all.

O Teacher, with Your Brilliance and Strength help us to prevail.

As our eyes gaze up toward You, unwavering,

We ask You to give to us, the withered and scorched, Your sweet dew,

So our roots of goodness are watered, grow thick and flourish.

～

O Holy Sage, Universal Lord, Messiah

We marvel at our Loving Father's Sea of Compassion.

From the humility of the Holy Sage to the essence of the Cool Wind,

All Dharma is bound together by Purity, nothing more, and cannot be attained through the mind.

The Story of Jesus

❀

The Sutras tell the story of Jesus simply and directly. They touch the important points, expressing them with a clarity not found in the traditional Gospels. They stress that Jesus proposed a way of life in tune with a vision of the spirit within life. The notion of the Tao shines through, not piercingly but subtly. Jesus doesn't represent the only route to spirituality, but he does embody the Tao, the nature of things, the way things are.

The moral teachings and miraculous healings of Jesus make sense because he represents both ordinary life and the great spirit. His work and life are sanctioned by the Cool Wind, a wonderfully sensuous image for the unnamable creating spirit. By now, having encountered wind as an image of spirit, we know enough to sense the spirituality in the image.

We also see that Jesus, who teaches the way of spirit, is misunderstood and feared by the scholars and those in power. He is innocent of any crime but is executed nevertheless. We know of a similar situation: Socrates, the teacher of wisdom, who was perceived as a threat to the Greek world.

The Eastern themes that give the Jesus of the Sutras both charm and an edge bring out certain essential elements in Christianity that might otherwise be overlooked. This Jesus is the embodiment of a way of being. He is not so much a moral teacher as an example of the healing power of spiritual existence. Having been acknowledged by the Cool Wind, he goes about a life of healing and teaching that has great power.

We know too well that to be dedicated to an open, tranquil life of spirit doesn't endear you to the world at large. You may be a threat to the status quo, perceived as a serious critic of institutions in which many have staked their lives. It's important to be ready, not only to be misunderstood but criticized as well. You may think honesty and moral vision will be rewarded, but the Jesus story makes it clear that deep morality easily falls victim to ideology and organization. You shouldn't be innocent as you display your religious sensibilities to a striving and competitive world.

~

The Lord of Heaven sent the Cool Wind to a girl named Mo Yen. It entered her womb and at that moment she conceived. The Lord of Heaven did this to show that conception could take place without a husband. He knew there was no man near her and that people who saw it would say, "How great is the power of the Lord of Heaven." Their hearts would become filled with pure faith and they would devote themselves to bettering the karmic condition of all.

Mo Yen became pregnant and gave birth to a son named Jesus, whose father is the Cool Wind. Some people were ignorant and said if she gave birth after becoming pregnant by the Cool Wind, then the whole thing was merely of this world. If a Sage on High issues an edict, then everyone willingly will submit to it. The Lord of Heaven dwells in heaven above and controls everything in heaven and earth.

When Jesus Messiah was born, the world saw clear signs in heaven and earth. A new star that could be seen everywhere appeared in heaven above. The star was as big as a cart wheel and shown brightly. At about this time, the One was born in the country of Ephrath in the city of Jerusalem. He was born the Messiah and after five years he began to preach the dharma. His message to all living creatures was to do good. When he was 12 years old he came to a purifying place called the Jordan in search of his spiritual nature. Together with the sage John he bathed in the waters. John lived in a rocky ravine and never drank alcohol or ate meat. He consumed only raw vegetables and honey gathered from the ground.

Many people came to this place to honor John and learn from him. When Jesus arrived, John led the Messiah to the Jordan to be baptized. After the Messiah had bathed and come out of the water, the Cool Wind came from heaven in the form of a dove and landed near the Messiah. A voice from the void spoke: "The Messiah is my son. All the living creatures in the world must obey him. His purpose is to do only good." The Messiah then showed everyone that the way of Heaven was to follow the Lord of Heaven. This meant that all living creatures in the world below must stop serving other gods. As soon as anyone heard these words, they must stop serving other gods, renounce evil and do good.

From the time the Messiah was 12 until he was 32 years old, he sought out people with bad karma and directed them to turn around and create good karma by following a wholesome path. After the Messiah had gathered 12 disciples, he concerned himself with the suffering of others. Those who had died were made to live. The blind were made to see. The deformed were healed and the sick were cured. The possessed were freed of their demons and the crippled were made to walk. People with all kinds of illnesses drew near to the Messiah to touch his ragged robe and be healed.

All those who do unwholesome deeds, who have not turned toward the path of goodness, who have no faith in the teaching of the Lord of Heaven, all those who are impure and covet profit, will never experience redemption.

The scribes who drank liquor and ate meat and served other gods brought false testimony against him. They waited for an opportunity to kill him. But many people had come to have faith in his teaching and so the scribes could not kill the Messiah. Eventually these people, whose karma was unwholesome, formed a conspiracy against him.

Pretending to be faithful and pure believers, they tried to kill the Messiah by legal means. But they could not find a way to do it, so they began to denounce him to the Great King. While these evil people plotted against him, the Messiah did good deeds and taught with even more vigor than before.

When the Messiah was 32 years old, his enemies came before the Great King Pilate and accused him by saying, The Messiah has committed a capital offense. The Great King should condemn him.

These people of unwholesome karma all testified in the presence of the Great King Pilate. The Great King, wanting to be just, reasoned that since he had not heard this person nor seen him, it would not be fitting that he should die. He said that the matter could be decided by the scribes themselves. The Great King said, "I cannot kill this man." And these people of unwholesome karma replied, if this man is not killed, think what will happen to us, men and women alike. The Great King Pilate asked for water and washed his hands. Then standing before the scribes and others in the crowd, he said that he had no reason to kill him. But the crowd pleaded its case over and over until his death became inevitable.

For the sake of all living beings and to show us that a human life is as frail as a candle flame, the Messiah gave his body to these people of unwholesome karma. For the sake of the living in this world, he gave up his life.

After the Messiah had accepted death, his enemies seized the Messiah and took him to a secluded spot, washed his hair and climbed to "the place of the skulls," which was called Golgotha. They bound him to a pole and placed two highway robbers to the right and left of him. They bound the Messiah to the pole at the time of the fifth watch of the sixth day of fasting. They bound him at dawn and when the sun set in the west the sky became black in all four directions, the earth quaked and the hills trembled. Tombs all over the world opened and the dead came to life. What person can see such a thing and not have faith in the teaching of the scriptures? To give one's life like the Messiah is a mark of great faith.

❧

PART THREE

The Soul of the Scrolls

Guidance for Today
from the 1300-year-old Teachings

The Tao of Jesus

❧

To know only one religion is to know none at all. The stories, devotions and sacred places of an unknown faith bring a richness and depth to our own beliefs. In the realm of the spirit, each tradition enhances the others. Unfortunately, many think of religions as exclusive organizations and systems of belief. We talk about ecumenism but don't take the next step to experience how a variety of religions can contribute to a full, complex spiritual life. The ancient Greeks sent observers to neighboring lands to study the ways of other spiritual communities and find ideas for their own practice. Perhaps it's time for us to do something similar and move forward from tolerance to reverence. The Jesus Sutras are an important compass to guide us along the way.

Throughout the history of religion, both accidental and intentional encounters have led communities to learn from one another and discover in the process that something new has been born. Zen arose out of such a meeting between Taoism and Buddhism, and 1300 years ago in China, Christianity mingled with Buddhism and Taoism to produce a fresh and enlightening new source of spiritual wisdom in the writings of Aleben and his later followers.

Though far apart in geography and language, the traditions of Occident and Orient have much in common, so it isn't surprising to see how beautifully they blend together in these unique texts. The Jesus of the Gospels teaches a life of peace, humility, paradox and egolessness. It's a short step to the Asian concepts of action through non-action and compassion through transcendence of the self. By taking Buddhist and Taoist teachings on yin and yang, the eternal law within things, and the search for an end to manic activity, and then combining them with the parables of Jesus, the Sutras create a more complex and deeply visionary form of Christianity.

Jesus in these "Christian Sutras" becomes more a teacher of wisdom than the focus of rigid beliefs that centuries of argument have made of him. The Buddhist influence in the texts further softens his presence and brings out the latent mystery that lies like a shadow in many of the biblical scenes of his teaching and healing. The biblical parable of a house built on sand becomes a lesson in mindfulness: "When we lack mindfulness," the Jesus of the Sutras tells us, "we are like someone who builds a house out of ignorance.... The wind comes and blows it away."

The Sutras provide us with a graphic image of the way to selflessness. Our hearts and minds, according to the texts, are not our own but are created by the winds. This is a typical Taoist use of nature to describe spiritual things and capture the idea of the no-self. The Holy Spirit becomes the Cool Wind, a more sensuous, evocative image for that which is invisible but felt. In mixing East and West, the Sutras take abstract teachings from the New Testament and give them a poetic resonance. They retain the ethical and intellectual dimension but add a wonderful element of sensuality.

As one passage from the Jesus Sutras relates, "We are always seeking and acting and because of this we create movement and desire, which cause unhappiness and make it difficult to attain Peace and Joy. Therefore I say we should live without desire and action." Anyone familiar with Taoism will recognize these ideas and understand that they do not imply passivity. It is the struggle to figure everything out that gets us in trouble. Particularly in passages like this, Jesus becomes a teacher of wisdom and compassion rather than a preacher concerned with sin and redemption. He offers ways to quiet the anxieties that erupt in aggression. By blending religious truths, the Sutras show how Jesus' teachings can easily be understood as "no desire." He did, after all, claim to be doing the will of his Heavenly Father, which is a different but complementary way of getting the ego out of the spiritual equation.

The Jesus Sutras might well be called "The Tao of Jesus." While his followers have often interpreted the Gospels as a fixed system of teachings and morals, the texts discovered in Dunhuang portray a spiritual leader who understands the interplay of yin and yang. Paradoxically, these foreign sutras present Jesus more faithfully than many Western interpretations. When he talks in the Sutras about "no desire," his lesson to those who are rejected and persecuted is to have faith in the truth and the redeeming power of emptiness, a key idea in both Taoism and Buddhism.

To those of us reading the Sutras today, religious emptiness can become not just a personal spiritual achievement but also a way of being in the world and dealing with our neighbors. To see value in the least of our brethren is to empty ourselves of a huge obstacle to spiritual maturity—the notion that only those who agree with us and share our beliefs are worthy of attention and admiration. What could be more empty, in the spiritual sense of being free of ambition and self-regard, than to love our enemies and be good to those who persecute us?

Key among the lessons for us to learn from this Tao of Jesus are its Four Essential Laws: no desire, no action, no virtue, and no truth. These teachings are difficult for the modern Westerner, who is full of craving and has often adopted a philosophy that doesn't provide a sense of belonging to the world community. For pleasure and meaning in today's society, we look to entertainment and science, two inadequate sources that only increase our craving. We are taught to be literal and constantly active. The Taoist ideal on the other hand is effortless action.

The Four Laws in the Jesus Sutras begin with no desire. This doesn't mean that you should once and for all purify yourself of all desire. That would be inhuman. But there is a kind of craving that can take away your freedom and tranquility, a compulsive sense of need—for things, food, people, money, sex and even experience. Strong desire can serve the spiritual life, but even the slightest degree of compulsion throws you off balance. Maybe you don't see the precious and beautiful life in front of you, and especially the simple and important things like children, family life, neighbors, nature and craft. Not having these things that enrich you at a deep level, you go after things that glitter without satisfying.

Second is the law of no action. Obviously, this doesn't mean becoming a vegetable. It means noticing the activities that keep you occupied but don't really make life worth living. Today everyone complains they're too busy, and yet the important things are not being done. We have many people in need of help. We need good storytelling, whether on television or in print. We need beautiful objects that are not mass-produced. We need supportive and safe cities and towns and food that doesn't poison us or cause disease. There is much for us to do, not for financial profit and personal enhancement, but to make life beautiful.

The spiritual enlightenment in the Sutras streams forth in their treatment of the third law, no virtue. Within the spiritual life there is an impulse toward sharing your excitement at finding insight and an effective way of life. But this natural desire to spread the word easily becomes excessive. In the extreme, believers force others to follow their way. In more modest form, the urge becomes an annoying attempt to convert others to your opinion.

The Jesus Sutras answer this by combining beliefs from Christianity, Taoism and Buddhism in a balanced and dynamic fashion. The result is a different form of piety, a devotion in which you focus on the wisdom and insight that has come to you. You may develop daily practices that keep your understanding in mind. This will lead in turn to serving not only the community that shares your vision but the greater community as well. All this is a form of piety that will do more to convince others of the value of your vision than any effort to convert and persuade.

The fourth law, no truth, can be a difficult one to accept. Think of it as the difference between fact and insight. We live in a culture that believes in provable facts. Anything else is personal, suspiciously subjective. Even in spiritual matters, you may think you possess the truth. But actually insight, with all its subjectivity, is more important than the illusion that you have all the answers. The word "truth" conveys the idea that you alone are aware of the ultimate reality. It is a highly dogmatic word, usually split off from the soul qualities that would temper it and make it less belligerent. The Jesus Sutras soften the notion of truth and give it a needed depth. In a society full of competitive claims about who is right, this slight change in attitude can inspire our religions and transform the way we lead our lives.

Lessons for Daily Living

⚗️

An important theme of the Jesus Sutras is the un-changing, eternal source of wisdom that is the One Spirit. Again and again, we are told how important it is to find right understanding, a basic Buddhist insight. It's easy to be led astray and fall into meaningless, if not outright evil, activities. The Sutras advise that we take the invisible and the timeless into account as we look for understanding, and that we pursue behavior that is not ambitious and full of striving.

Ego, psychology, practicality and self-interest will not take you where you want to go. Through these modernist values you will only find frustration. Indeed, they are the roots of neurosis and personal frustration. They are not big enough. They don't take into account the vast myste-riousness of nature, of which you are a part. To fulfill the material of your own nature, you need a spiritual viewpoint, a constant contact with origins, the holy winds, and the laws exemplified in the natural world.

Many modern people seek some form of spirituality out of their confusion and sense of meaninglessness. But they often approach new spiritual resources with old, modernist values. They may link their spiritual efforts to their fitness programs or imagine spirituality within the context of therapeutics, which is a dominant attitude in our times.

The Jesus Sutras are not another form of self-realization or therapy. They are aimed at a deep level of compassion that affects life everywhere—other people and the things of nature and culture. These texts go beyond therapy, offering a way of being that is rooted in the natural laws of yin and yang and mutual dependence. They suggest a way out of the maddening cycles of work, failed relationships, illness and loneliness that characterize much of modern life.

The contemporary person has lost sight of the eternal, the original and the mysterious. Everything is a problem to be solved. Happiness is imagined in terms of money and prestige. Today the capital sin of envy takes the form of celebrity worship. All this suggests that the modern person doesn't enjoy a deep source of tranquility and emotional peace. People strive for satisfaction in the extraordinary conditions of wealth and fame rather than in the ordinary and natural pleasures of friendship and connection.

text continued on page 134

Our Personal Sutras

~

The word "sutra," derived from a Sanskrit term for thread, is more than a brief aphoristic teaching. It is quite literally a thread—a way, a path to be followed. Throughout the Jesus Sutras there are numbered "lessons"—the Four Laws of the Dharma, the Ten Methods for Meditating on the World, and so on. These can be read as spiritual literature, but they also can be used as teaching guides, step-by-step principles to follow when we are in the midst of the challenges and decisions of everyday life.

They guide us toward a philosophy of life, which is a central achievement in any spiritual path. As an art of memory, reading these Sutras educates the spiritual imagination. Not only are the numbered lessons and key words helpful for memory, they penetrate deep into the heart, more so perhaps than extended and more complicated explorations of belief.

The subtle yet powerful mixture of Christian, Buddhist and Taoist wisdom in the Jesus Sutras may, however, present a special challenge. You will probably not find in your vicinity a single community that simultaneously embraces all these religions. You may be devoted to life as a Christian or perhaps a Jew or Buddhist. In any case, you will have to decide how to live this new, enlightening, blended spirituality. You will have to make it your own: and that is one of its benefits. But it's impossible to be a passive recipient of these teachings. By their very nature they demand that you adopt a way of thinking and living that melds the traditions into something new and unique.

You have to appropriate these Sutras as your own. In doing so you need not fear any threat to your current beliefs and attachments. You don't have to become a Taoist/Christian/Buddhist hybrid to profit from these teachings. They invite us to add a new dimension to our spiritual life, and in so doing they become our sutras, to express, interpret and embody in ways we see fit.

As one sutra instructs, "Those who have compassion for other creatures and act in this way without seeking praise are true to their own hearts.... Ultimately it leads them along the Way of Peace and Joy to enlightenment." The point is to stay attuned to the mysterious law coursing through you and your life. Be religious and spiritual but don't get caught in empty outward forms. When you are attuned to the deep laws of your nature, you can trust your heart. Today people find it difficult to trust themselves. Often their cravings and understandings only get them into trouble. They come to mistrust their deep intuitions and judgments.

One solution, exemplified in the Eastern and Western blend of these texts, is to learn the laws of your nature from the ways of the natural world. Find your place in nature and live from that sense of support and harmony. The Jesus Sutras say: "The sky is in love with you. The earth opens its arms in peace." These words are addressed to the Compassionate Father, making the all-important connection between this concrete world and the Sacred Spirit. They also apply to you: The skies love you and the earth gives you its support.

In the Sutras, the winds give you your identity and the sun reminds you of the luminous way you can re-fashion that identity. Nature is the great teacher, the book of life to be read and understood. That's why it is important not just to protect the natural world, but to guide it to the highest level of perfection. Our task as spiritual people is to foster an intimate bond between the world of nature—rivers, mountains, oceans, animals, forests—and our own felt nature. When one is thriving, the other will find needed support. The great mystery of these Sutras is that the realm of the sensuous is identical with the world of spirit.

At the top of the great Monument Sutra in Xian stands the powerful image of the cross emerging out of the lotus. This stele not only portrays the inspiring notion of one religion rooted in another, it also conveys the equally important idea that the world of the senses gives rise to the visionary realm of spiritual awareness. You can't have one without the other.

This mystery plays out in our personal, daily lives. Living in the lotus of body and the sensuous world, we become people of exquisite vision and virtue. Here, virtue means quality and depth of life, not moralistic perfection. That is the gift of the lotus, to ground our ideas of spiritual achievement in the beauty of ordinary life. The lotus humanizes, the cross inspires us toward unlimited compassion.

In this way the Jesus Sutras correct the modern tendency to make spirituality too precious and too removed from the ordinary joys and travails of getting along, and to make ordinary life too personal, too materialistic and largely unconscious. What Buddhism and Taoism have done for the Gospel teachings in these Sutras, other religions can do for each other. Perhaps we will find more lost texts that have blossomed at that point where, with a degree of innocence, one religion brings out the best in another.

People sometimes ask what religion will look like in the future. The Jesus Sutras provide a clue. They show how religions can encounter each other and produce a new, vivifying vision. People also ask what psychology might be like in a hundred years or so. The Sutras suggest that it may disappear, along with other inadequate institutions created by twentieth-century modernism. In its place we may find a highly livable, individual, reverent way of life in which the religious traditions all contribute. With the best of hopes, we will honor each other, as the winds, and especially the Cool Wind, give us our identity and purpose.

Bibliography

❧

Bernstein, Richard. *Ultimate Journey: Retracing the Path of an Ancient Buddhist Monk Who Crossed Asia in Search of Enlightenment.* New York: Vintage Departures, 2002.

Bonavia, Judy. *The Silk Road: From Xi'an to Kashgar,* 6th ed. Hong Kong: Airphoto International, 2002.

Buck, Pearl. Introduction to *The Sacred Oasis: Caves of the Thousand Buddhas, Tun Huang,* by Irene Vongher Vincent. London: Farber and Farber, [no date].

Carus, Paul, editor. *The Nestorian Monument: An Ancient Record of Christianity in China.* Chicago: The Open Court Publishing Company, 1909.

Chiu, Peter C. H. *An Historical Study of Nestorian Christianity in the T'ang Dynasty Between A. D. 635-845.* Fort Worth: Southwestern Baptist Theological Seminary, 1987.

Gillman, Ian, and Hans-Joachim Klimkeit. *Christians in Asia before 1500.* Ann Arbor: University of Michigan Press, 1999.

Hopkirk, Peter. *Foreign Devils on the Silk Road: The Search for the Lost Cities and Treasures of Chinese Central Asia.* Amherst: The University of Massachusetts Press, 1980.

Hui Li. *The Life of Hieun Tsiang.* Westport, CT: Hyperion Press, 1973.

Li, Dun J. *The Ageless Chinese: A History.* New York: Charles Scriber's Sons, 1965.

Moffett, Samuel Hugh. *A History of Christianity in Asia. Volume One: Beginnings to 1500.* San Francisco: HarperSanFrancisco, 1992.

Moule, A.C. *Christians in China before the Year 1550.* New York: Society for Promoting Christian Knowledge, Macmillan Co., 1930.

Neill, Stephen. *Christian Missions.* Harmondsworth, Middlesex: Penguin Books, 1964.

Palmer, Martin. *The Jesus Sutras: Rediscovering the Lost Scrolls of Taoist Christianity.* New York: Ballantine Wellspring, 2001.

Saeki, P.Y. *Catalogue of The Nestorian Literature and Relics.* Tokyo: Maruzen, 1950.

——————. *The Nestorian Documents and Relics in China.* Tokyo: Maruzen Company Ltd., 1951

Whitfield, Roderick, Susan Whitfield and Neville
    Agnew. *Cave Temples of Mogao: Art and History on the
    Silk Road*. Los Angeles: The J. Paul Getty Trust, 2000.
Whitfield, Susan. *Life Along the Silk Road*. Berkeley:
    University of California Press, 1999.

About the Editors

❧

THOMAS MOORE is the author of several bestselling books, including *Care of the Soul* and *The Soul's Religion*. Also a psychotherapist and lecturer, he resides in New Hampshire with his wife and two children. He lived as a monk in a Catholic religious order for 12 years and received a Ph.D. in religious study from Syracuse University.

RAY RIEGERT is the co-author of the *Gospel of Thomas* and editor of *The Lost Gospel Q* and *Jesus and Buddha: The Parallel Sayings*. A member of the Society of Biblical Literature and the American Association of Religion, he lives in Berkeley, California, with his wife and two children.